## About Demos

*Who we are*

Demos is the think tank for everyday democracy. We believe everyone should be able to make personal choices in their daily lives that contribute to the common good. Our aim is to put this democratic idea into practice by working with organisations in ways that make them more effective and legitimate.

*What we work on*

We focus on six areas: public services; science and technology; cities and public space; people and communities; arts and culture; and global security.

*Who we work with*

Our partners include policy-makers, companies, public service providers and social entrepreneurs. Demos is not linked to any party but we work with politicians across political divides. Our international network – which extends across Eastern Europe, Scandinavia, Australia, Brazil, India and China – provides a global perspective and enables us to work across borders.

*How we work*

Demos knows the importance of learning from experience. We test and improve our ideas in practice by working with people who can make change happen. Our collaborative approach means that our partners share in the creation and ownership of new ideas.

*What we offer*

We analyse social and political change, which we connect to innovation and learning in organisations. We help our partners show thought leadership and respond to emerging policy challenges.

*How we communicate*

As an independent voice, we can create debates that lead to real change. We use the media, public events, workshops and publications to communicate our ideas. All our books can be downloaded free from the Demos website.

**www.demos.co.uk**

First published in 2006
© Demos
Some rights reserved – see copyright licence for details

ISBN 1 84180 158 5
Copy edited by Julie Pickard
Typeset by utimestwo, Collingtree, Northants
Printed in the UK

For further information and
subscription details please contact:

Demos
Magdalen House
136 Tooley Street
London SE1 2TU

telephone:  0845 458 5949
email:  hello@demos.co.uk
web:  www.demos.co.uk

# The Other Glass Ceiling

## The domestic politics of parenting

Hannah Green
Sophia Parker

# DEM©S

**Open access. Some rights reserved.**

As the publisher of this work, Demos has an open access policy which enables anyone to access our content electronically without charge.

We want to encourage the circulation of our work as widely as possible without affecting the ownership of the copyright, which remains with the copyright holder.

Users are welcome to download, save, perform or distribute this work electronically or in any other format, including in foreign language translation, without written permission subject to the conditions set out in the Demos open access licence which you can read at the back of this publication.

Please read and consider the full licence. The following are some of the conditions imposed by the licence:

- Demos and the author(s) are credited
- The Demos website address (www.demos.co.uk) is published together with a copy of this policy statement in a prominent position
- The text is not altered and is used in full (the use of extracts under existing fair usage rights is not affected by this condition)
- The work is not resold
- A copy of the work or link to its use online is sent to the address below for our archive.

Copyright Department
Demos
Magdalen House
136 Tooley Street
London
SE1 2TU
United Kingdom

copyright@demos.co.uk

You are welcome to ask for permission to use this work for purposes other than those covered by the Demos open access licence.

## ©creative commons

Demos gratefully acknowledges the work of Lawrence Lessig and Creative Commons which inspired our approach to copyright. The Demos circulation licence is adapted from the 'attribution/no derivatives/non-commercial' version of the Creative Commons licence.

To find out more about Creative Commons licences go to www.creativecommons.org

# Contents

|  | | |
|---|---|---|
| | Acknowledgements | 7 |
| | Foreword | 9 |
| | Executive summary | 12 |
| 1. | Why families matter | 21 |
| 2. | Getting behind the front door: a typology of everyday family life | 32 |
| 3. | Paid work: what is productive? | 51 |
| 4. | Mum's the word: the other glass ceiling | 63 |
| 5. | Public value, private responsibility? | 77 |
| 6. | Opening up the scripts of family life: recommendations | 85 |
| 7. | Endnote: where next for work–life balance debates? | 104 |
| | Appendices | |
| | A. List of project interviews | 108 |
| | B. List of attendees at the project seminar | 109 |
| | C. The research process | 110 |
| | Notes | 112 |

# Acknowledgements

This publication would not have been possible without the financial support of Sanofi Pasteur MSD. Munro and Forster have also played a key role in making this publication happen. We would particularly like to thank Dave Roberts and Efe Abebe.

We are especially grateful to Gillian Thomas for her invaluable contribution to the research process and to Celia Hannon for her exhaustive research, comments and reflections at every stage.

At Demos our thanks go to all our colleagues who helped us to frame this project. Special mentions should go to Sarah Gillinson for her help during the course of the research, to John Craig for his thoughtful comments throughout the process and to Tom Bentley who gave us invaluable intellectual challenge and insight during the writing process. Thanks also to Sam Hinton-Smith for his media work and Julia Huber who saw the text safely through to production and publication.

We are indebted to many individuals who contributed to our research through participating in interviews and focus groups, speaking at seminars and being on hand to offer advice. For a full list please see appendix A but here we would particularly like to thank Mary Crowley, Sally Russell, Matthew Horne, Jenny Watson, Kathleen Healy, Duncan Fisher, Susan Hay, Naomi Eisenstadt and Gwen Vaughn.

Thanks should also go to all the families who helped the research by talking to us and filling in diaries and to Sarah Ellis from the National Day Nurseries Association for recruiting and hosting focus groups.

Finally we would like to thank John and Dave for doing the 'double shift' during this project.

As ever, all errors and omissions remain our own.

Hannah Green  
Sophia Parker  
April 2006

# Foreword

## Jenny Watson

Thirty years on from the Sex Discrimination Act feels like a good time to take stock of where we are, one generation in, and look at the next steps of the sex equality journey. There have been some fantastic leaps forward: women are increasingly economically independent and with that has come a sense of greater freedom socially and culturally.

But in achieving the amazing things that we have – it is no small measure of work to make it possible for women to live as men do – a great part of human existence has been hidden: family activity (traditionally private) has taken place out of public space, out of public sight. We cannot truly achieve sex equality unless we refashion a society which can cope with the whole of that human existence, which can give space for our important human relationships and the time, effort and energy that they demand. We need to re-start what some have described as the stalled gender revolution.

Men's lives are changing too, with an increasing number of dads – especially young fathers – expressing the desire to spend more time with their children. This remains a quiet revolution, easy to miss because it takes place in people's homes, behind people's front doors, up and down the country. Nevertheless, these shifts represent a tipping point – where change of a qualitatively different nature becomes both possible and necessary. It is like moving from a two-dimensional model which looks at equality between men and women, and adding an explicit third dimension – that of family and care.

As this report demonstrates, for families themselves, this third dimension is at the heart of who they are. It is now urgent for political parties concerned about their own survival to address these issues and catch up with the views expressed by the families in this report. In some polling we conducted at the Equal Opportunities Commission (EOC), we discovered that 70% of people were concerned about what family life will be like for their children and grandchildren; nearly half were very concerned.

Decisions about our home life and how we run it will always remain private. But these decisions also need to be reflected in public policy debate – debate about what legal infrastructure, what public policy levers can best support families of all kinds; about how we invest in public services that can support every element of the family: mothers, fathers, children and older and disabled people. Put bluntly, our own individual choices are decisions we now expect to make in the context of supportive, enabling public service, and against a more sophisticated framework of employment rights which recognises that men, as well as women, want to balance work and home life – and not pay a poverty penalty for the choices they have made.

What will this involve? I believe the analysis and recommendations of this report give some strong indications of the kind of approach that will be required to make the next great leap in debates about gender equality. The most promising sign – but perhaps also the most difficult area to debate publicly – is men and women working together to negotiate about their lives. The suggestion in this report that gender equality debates need to be strongly connected to the quality of life agenda is a powerful one: people need to see that they are not alone in wanting a different way to share home and life.

The area where there is most to do is the interaction between paid and unpaid work, what is valued and how. We need to think about a whole new ideal of care, an ideal that sees care as a positive contribution to society. This in turn needs to be supported by an infrastructure designed to help families care, rather than an approach focused on outsourcing such important work. Our relationships, as the bedrock of secure families, are crucial, and our public life needs to be shaped round these, rather than the other way round.

By producing a report grounded in the everyday lives of hardworking families, rather than abstract statistics or policy frameworks, Demos has made a crucial and incisive contribution to the debate. This pamphlet demonstrates that there is more work to be done than many think. Our challenge is to lift legal and attitudinal barriers that prevent us, as human beings rather than stereotypically portrayed men and women, from making the choices that we wish to make, and being treated with respect and dignity when we do. That is the challenge we now face. It is a challenge that the EOC is working hard to address. I do hope many more voices will join us in the campaign to address the imbalance in value currently afforded to paid and unpaid work.

*Jenny Watson is Chair of the Equal Opportunities Commission.*

# Executive summary

People always say that the family is never what it once was. For too long debates about family life and work–life balance have focused on what families look like, rather than asking a more challenging set of questions about what families are for and why they matter. Despite proclamations that the family is in terminal decline, there is evidence that the aspiration to be a 'good family' is in fact becoming more significant – for individuals, government and indeed society more generally.

In this context, there is a real need to describe and recognise the fact that the work parents do in raising children does not simply benefit those individual children; there is a *public value* to parenting that so far has remained unrecognised and trapped behind people's front doors.

This report examines the everyday life of the 'hard-working families' who have recently become so popular in political debate. Drawing on original research as well as existing data, we frame a new agenda for debate about family life: an agenda that argues it is in the public interest to recognise and strengthen the relationships between families, state and civil society.

Rather than focusing on moralising arguments about the significance of changing family structures, this report explores the many ways in which families work to combine a whole host of activities – including paid employment and unpaid care work – to maximise the life chances of their children. This pamphlet does not endorse a single family type to the exclusion of others. Chapter 1 opens up a debate about why families, whatever their shape or size, matter. In chapter 2 we develop a typology that describes and analyses some of the ways in which families adapt to the challenge of integrating employment and family life. Many families will go through a number of the types we have identified over the course of time.

This illustrative typology grew out of our original research. We began by identifying pinch points in family life, or times that families found particularly stressful. These included when the first child was born; when a child had a contagious illness and standard childcare arrangements broke down; when a child started school; when a second or subsequent child was born; and when parents took on additional caring responsibilities, for example looking after their own parents.

Using these pinch points to bring into sharp relief the delicacy of the support structures that families build around themselves as part of day-to-day life, we then conducted some in-depth interviews in a number of families' homes to enrich our understanding of the ways in which families are adapting to the challenge of combining paid and unpaid work.

The typology is not about describing a hierarchy, or 'right' and 'wrong' ways of organising family life. Rather, it points to the need to better understand the cast of characters we have identified, in order to strengthen the connections between the families that exist and approaches to designing support to help people give their children the best possible start in life.

### The art of motherhood – 'Mum's the word'

The mother in this family will dominate the domestic environment and hold the reins of family life. The father is likely to fulfil a traditional male breadwinner role; if the mother works she will probably have a locally based job in the childcare sector. Mums do not define themselves by their job, instead vesting their identity in childrearing and homemaking. This may be because women found that the jobs on offer to them as mums were less creative and stimulating than being a mother, or because motherhood was an active choice. Either way, the allocation of unpaid care falls almost entirely on the mother, but this is by mutual agreement. Men and women are seen to be equally important to family life, but their contributions are different and defined by their gender.

### Frustrated feminists – 'If you can't beat them, join them'

These families are made up of couples who expected they would be able to balance the arrival of children with their jobs successfully, but have been thwarted in their efforts to maintain an equitable split of unpaid care work. Both parents end up feeling stressed out and tired as they continue to try to both work hard and be active parents. Sometimes mothers will 'opt-out' of organisations entirely in order to set up their own enterprises in an attempt to find a more satisfying balance of home and work. Fathers will often feel uncertain of their identity as parents, having expected family life to be more straightforward than it turned out to be, and much as they love their children, will hark back to the easier life of pre-children years.

### Domestic democracy – 'We've come a long way, baby'

These families are unusual and they know it. They self-consciously and continually negotiate with each other about who does what in family life. Many will be in careers they enjoy, with good flexible arrangements; often these families will list their employers as important sources of support. They are experts at juggling, and will often outsource elements of childcare or housework in recognition of the importance of 'quality time' both with their children and each other. Often this state of affairs grows out of some kind of crisis where families have been forced to challenge the way they do things and to reassess their priorities.

## Executive summary

### Everybody needs good neighbours – 'You want to go where everybody knows your name'

These families describe themselves as 'very typical'. Both parents characterise their work as jobs rather than careers. They live their lives in narrow but comfortable horizons. The parents are likely to have met locally and feel a sense of shared history and values. They will have a strong relationship with where they live and take pleasure from living near similar kinds of people. They will have a tight-knit network of extended family and friends close by who form an important element of family life. Both parents are likely to give and receive support from this network.

### Keep it in the family – 'The family that eats together, stays together'

Unlike our 'everybody needs good neighbours' families, this type will see the front door as a firm boundary between family life and the wider world, which is perceived as potentially disruptive or threatening to the natural order of things. They see themselves as an independent unit and are proud of their self-sufficiency. They are likely to base their family organisation on the way that their parents did it and fall back on traditional and familiar ideas as anchors in the face of change. Mothers are likely to play a more active role in family life than fathers, but both parents will make the effort to spend time as a family unit on a regular basis.

### What money can buy – 'You can't buy love, but for everything else there's MasterCard'

These families have found a way to balance life at a price that most people can't afford – by outsourcing their childcare, cleaning and day-to-day management of their family home. Unlike the domestically democratic households, these families are unlikely to list their employers as sources of support. In other words, this is not just about straightforward consumerism: time is a commodity for these parents as well, and this type is interested in 'buying' quality time. Parents in these families aspire to a certain lifestyle that they are not willing to sacrifice. But they also want to ensure that their limited time is spent focusing on their children, for whom they prioritise learning and development within a structured environment.

### The survivors – 'Getting by matters more than getting on'

These parents are both working incredibly hard to do whatever is necessary to care for and keep their family going. Many parents in this category find themselves in 'flexible' shift work, although often they are holding down more than one job to keep food on the table and the bills paid. Choice is not discussed: parents are focused entirely on keeping things going. It is not so much the children who suffer from these arrangements but the parents. Between working and childcare, shifts and sleep, parents often see very little of each other. Often the second wage in this family type is negated by the cost of childcare, meaning that parents are likely to work part-time or on shifts.

These seven family types demonstrate that every household adapts to the challenge of juggling paid work and unpaid care to meet the needs of their children in different ways. But families do not organise the range of resources they have – economic, emotional, social, cultural, personal and physical – in splendid isolation. Their decisions about how to bring up their children are influenced by a host of social, cultural and institutional realities.

Although this report argues that families themselves are in the best position to judge how to bring up their children, we also explore the fact that often these external factors constrain the choices parents feel able to make about how they can best combine paid and unpaid work. Chapters 3, 4 and 5 explore the *dynamic interchange* between these wider factors and patterns of everyday family life. These include the following.

### An assumption that paid work alone is the priority

The norm in modern families is for both parents to work, and to be working harder than ever before. This is not at the cost of their

## Executive summary

children, but at the cost of their own time and time with their partner. Men and women alike emphasise the equal importance of paid and unpaid work to family life, but this parity remains unrecognised by mainstream debate and policy formulation. A progressive politics for families needs to keep productivity in perspective by shining a light on the hidden value of the unpaid care that goes into raising future generations. This unpaid work deserves equal prominence to questions about making paid work better for parents in the debate about how best to support families.

### Ongoing nature of gendered labour market and the other glass ceiling

Women continue to take greater responsibility than men for family and home life. Although gendered roles within the home are normalised by parents, they are in fact the product of a wider set of cultural, social and institutional patterns that individual families find impossible to overcome alone. These patterns thwart the desires of women, and increasingly men, to allocate family resources in a more equal and negotiated way. The challenge remains to find ways of ensuring that it is children's outcomes and the public value created by family life that drive the distribution of family activity, rather than these entrenched gendered attitudes.

### A decline in support – both formal and informal – for families in creating public value

We are expecting families to bring up their children with less and less support, informal and formal, from wider society. At the same time parents are feeling under greater pressure to be perfect parents. This has led to a stalemate: parents are stressed and lonely; the state is wary of intervening in the subtle dynamics of family life. Yet there are gains to be won for family, state and civil society if the relationships between these elements of the social fabric are strengthened. The challenge rests in casting the relationship in such a way that privacy is respected, but not at the expense of giving children the best start in life.

To fully release the public value that families could create for the whole of society, new ways need to be found to support families in the creation of that value, through forms of positive support, and through efforts to remove some of the barriers to families making decisions that are based on the best interests of their children. Chapter 6 maps out what this new landscape of support might look like.

What makes this agenda more complex is the fact that families access support from a range of formal and informal sources each day. In these terms, government cannot 'deliver' the public value of families. Instead, a series of shifts are needed – changes in institutional patterns, existing public services, the respective role of employers and the media – to create a culture that recognises the value that families create for everyone, and a society that proactively supports people in bringing up their children.

We argue that, in order to achieve this kind of change, 'public service' needs to be reconceived as *helping people to help themselves.* Good services need to involve people in conversations to understand their wants and uncover their needs. Reflecting a long tradition in progressive politics, the prize is less about creating a perfect set of public service institutions, and more about how services can help people to transform their lives and, ultimately, themselves. State, civil society and families need to work together to co-produce the kinds of goods – health, empowerment, future citizens, social capital – that bind people together.

In these terms, our recommendations represent a set of 'design principles': aspirations that can be used to drive change at every point of the systems in which families operate. The recommendations are therefore applicable to a range of players, from government and policy-makers to local service providers, voluntary organisations and employers.

This will not be achieved by a single or simple policy intervention. This agenda demands a different kind of political leadership: one based on articulating values and vision, even if politicians and policy-makers alone cannot enact the changes this report argues are

## Executive summary

necessary. State, employers and families must learn to work together. Within this context our recommendations are as follows.

### Start with families themselves in designing and delivering support

The state cannot remain neutral in family life. However, intervention does not need to add up to intrusion. The government should experiment in new mechanisms to encourage a shift in public culture and to support families in making the best possible choices for their children in the organisation of family life. Some examples include investing in 'family life' vouchers to provide support for families in the home, and developing a new framework for the inspection of childcare based on public value. Employers should also be encouraged to recast the workplace as part of the extended family rather than a 'home-from-home' to better align with the stated desires of families. One step would be for employers to fund networks of childminders in the home, rather than invest in workplace nursery facilities.

### Open up a public conversation about parenting

The popularity of television programmes such as *Wifeswap* and *Supernanny* have offered a unique opportunity to look inside and learn from other families. Broadcasters should be encouraged to develop similar formats, and public services should learn how the experiences of such television programmes can be transferred into public policy and used to support family life.

### Build negotiating capacity within families through peer support

Parents believe that being a parent, not training as an adviser, is what makes people 'experts' in family life. Policy-makers should foster the development of networks that provide learning opportunities and enable parents to support each other. These include online communities such as Netmums as well as other more locally based initiatives.

### Invest in quality relationships

The quality of parental relationships has an impact on children's lives. Modern relationships face a challenging range of pressures and yet support is rarely on offer until a relationship has reached crisis. Quality advice coupled with work, patience and self-awareness (rather than the idealised media representation of romantic love) can be the secret to maintaining success. In the face of weakening extended family bonds and community networks, government should increase financial support to organisations working on relationships and family support, and make private relationship counselling tax deductible.

### Involve fathers

While dads need to be fully engaged in family life at an early stage, there remain too few opportunities for men to express their desires beyond the household. The research conducted for this report indicates that children's health is an area where men are getting increasingly involved. Focusing on areas of family life where men are already involved is a promising start. Equally, as a further step in the right direction, all schools should run a 'take your dad to school' day to encourage fathers to play an active role in parenting and learning. This is about increasing the number of regular, everyday interactions on offer to fathers, rather than taking a 'big bang' approach.

### Experiment at work

Enabling people to balance work and home life is one of the most effective routes to releasing their potential. Employers should be encouraged to experiment in new ways of enabling flexible working, so that it means far more than simply working 'part-time'. There are also important lessons to be learned from 'enterprise mums' – the growing number of women who have 'opted out' to set up their own businesses, often in the childcare sector, as a way of achieving more control over the balance between work and life.

# 1. Why families matter

Families matter, not only to the individuals in them, but also to society. But society is putting parents under greater pressure, to be both economically productive *and* to produce healthy and happy future citizens. This report focuses on the 'hard-working families' so popular in current debate. Drawing on original research as well as existing data, we explore the domestic politics of parenting and frame a new agenda for debate about family life: an agenda that argues it is in the public interest to recognise and strengthen the relationships between families, state and civil society.

There has long been a nervousness about intervening or even commenting on the nature of family life unless parents find themselves in crisis or their children are at risk. Too often interventions make assumptions about the relationship between particular kinds of family formation and the success of parents in raising their children.

In this pamphlet, we argue that when it comes to families, the focus should be on function not form. In other words, there should be less interest in particular family formations or structures, and much more concern about the extent to which modern families are able to combine a whole host of activities – including both paid employment and unpaid care work – to maximise the life chances of their children. While the right to a private family life is one that should be jealously guarded, the wariness in talking about everyday family patterns has skewed the debate. It has hidden the fact that what families do is of *public value* as well as of benefit to individuals.

This report aims to refocus the debate on this question of the ways in which families combine paid and unpaid work. The typology of family life we have developed in chapter 2 indicates that families have a range of adaptive responses to the challenge of integrating employment and family life.

While it is undoubtedly true that every family strives to find satisfactory ways to organise and manage their shared life, the foundations on which their decisions are made have not been formed in splendid isolation. The way families organise themselves is influenced by myriad social, cultural and institutional factors that build up a web of family values. As this report documents, it is still too often the case that family responses are shaped by these cultural legacies and external drivers, rather than by the best interests of the children. Chapters 3, 4 and 5 explore the impact of some of these issues on everyday family life.

To fully release the public value that families could create for the whole of society, new ways need to be found to support families in the creation of that value, through forms of positive support, and through efforts to remove some of the existing barriers to families making decisions that are based on the best interests of their children. Chapter 6 maps out what this new landscape of support might look like.

Families access support from a range of formal and informal sources every day. Government cannot 'deliver' the public value of family life through a simple or single intervention. Rather, a series of shifts are needed – in institutional patterns, the way 'public service' is understood, the role of employers and the media – to create a culture and society that not only recognises the value that families create for everyone, but also proactively supports people in bringing up their children.

In starting with the experiences of families themselves, this report indicates that there is much to be learned from how parents are juggling all their resources – economic, social, cultural, personal and physical – to create the best possible life chances for their children. What our research suggests is that in trying to solve the immediate challenges of work and family life, people are beginning to generate some new answers to much deeper questions about what kind of lives we want to lead. It is these insights, rather than an overly simple focus on productivity or family structures alone, that need to drive the next wave of debate around the importance of family life.

**The family is dead; long live the family**
The lament of every generation – that families aren't what they were – is so familiar that it is rendered meaningless. Families are never what they were. The debate about family life has long been focused on what families look like, how they are composed and the formal relationships that bind them together. It's certainly true that marriage no longer has the place it once did in family life: people are less concerned about marriage and they don't see it as the bedrock of being a good family. The number of divorces is rising year on year and the number of children being born outside marriage is increasing. Two and a half million kids are involved in step-family life, which is the fastest-growing family form in the UK.

But none of this implies that the *aspiration* to create a family has declined. It's just that 'family' is an elastic term. Despite dire predictions of the 'back to basics' observers, the decline of marriage has not led to the dissolution of social networks and the emergence of a self-serving and lonely society of individuals.

The focus of the debate on the changing nature of family structures has eclipsed a much more interesting set of questions. What are families for? Why do they matter? How can they best be supported by the state, employers and others? It is these questions that this pamphlet is focused on. We aim to answer them through starting with the attitudes and behaviours of families themselves.

The more interesting trends that provide a context for this work centre on an apparent *growth*, rather than decline, in the importance of family life. This growth is played out at individual family levels, in the focus of policy and indeed in our society, media and culture more generally. Increasingly, mothers and fathers are seeking to attain the goal of 'perfect parenting'. Yet as parents are bombarded with a host of 'how to' guides in books, TV shows and magazines we may well be witnessing the emergence of 'paranoid parents'.

Despite more parents working,[1] and working more hours, they are spending longer on childrearing activities each day than ever before. In 1981 dads with a partner in full-time employment spent an average of 17 hours a week with their children; by 1997 the equivalent group were putting in 23 hours of time with their children each week.[2] The time spent by working mothers with their children has also grown over the last two decades, from less than 40 minutes per day in 1974–5 to over 90 minutes in 1999. Indeed, working mothers spend more time with their children now than non-working mothers did in 1981.[3] There has also been a rise in the number of families eating a home-cooked dinner together every night from 12 per cent in 1961 to 19 per cent in 2001.[4] One British study found that in affluent two-children families, parents are coordinating an average of eight to ten activities a week for their offspring.[5] So parents are increasingly making time to spend with their children.

But it is not just individuals who continue to believe in the importance of the family. In recent years there has been a wider cultural shift in the way that parenting activity is viewed; it is moving from being a private family matter to an issue that is a legitimate subject for public debate. The explosion in parenting programmes – such as *Supernanny*, *Nanny 911* and *Wifeswap* – which have replaced property shows as the must-have format for every channel, combined with the bewildering array of books, magazines and gurus offering advice, suggests that parents are working harder than ever to become 'professional' parents who know more and more about what good childrearing is.

Policy is beginning to catch up with this renewed focus on the importance of family life. Recent developments in education, the 'Respect' agenda and the Children Act all reflect a growing interest within government about the significance of families. There is a recognition that families could potentially play a pivotal role in achieving some of the ambitious goals around reducing social exclusion, and in particular child poverty, and giving everyone an equal chance in life. The question is *how* government will translate this renewed commitment to families into forms of support that are meaningful and go with the grain of what parents and children want and need. Although there is not yet a coherent policy story about families, parenting and children, the renewed emphasis on supporting 'hard-working families' reflects a desire in government to find new ways of achieving some of these goals.

## What are families for?

It is often argued by historians and social commentators that the Industrial Revolution led to a transformation in family life. Technological changes, coupled with cultural shifts, led to the emergence of separated 'public' and 'private' spheres. Men became the custodians of the worlds of business, commerce and politics; work was driven out of homes and into the factory, creating new categories of productive and reproductive work. Women became embedded in a household focused on reproduction. In other words, modern capitalism has constructed the modern family as a private realm closed from scrutiny, a retreat from the world. It also served to emphasise the concept of 'childhood'. Rather than children being seen as potential contributors to the family economy, they were seen as passive family members in need of nurture, education and love.

There are some indications that family life really is more privatised. People are spending more time in their homes.[6] Children are taking longer to leave home.[7] The 2002 *Social Trends* survey found that nearly a third of men aged between 20 and 35 live with their parents, compared with only one in four in 1977–8. In July 2001, a study commissioned by Abbey National confirmed this claim, and pointed out that the proportion of young adults who return home after initially fleeing the nest has nearly doubled from 25 per cent in 1950 to 46 per cent today.

As we have already noted, parents are spending more time with their children now than they were 30 years ago – at the expense of relationship and 'me' time.[8] The decline in informal and community-based forms of support to families, explored further in chapter 5, means that families are increasingly reliant on themselves alone to bring up their children. As Shirley Burggraf pointed out, 'no society until recent times has expected love alone to support the family enterprise. To put it another way, parental love has never cost so much'.[9]

In other words, childrearing, rather than formal relationship bonds or extended family networks, is the focus of modern families. The growing diversity of family forms and bonds does not detract from the fact that the family remains the most fundamental social unit and is still the most important thing in children's lives.

For the vast majority of children, families are the places where they are looked after, protected and fed. Families are the primary site for the production of values, beliefs and worldviews. They will determine to a significant extent the ways in which we relate to the world around us.

In thinking about what families are for, it is possible to group activities under four headings.

### Basic needs
Basic needs include cleanliness, health, shelter and nourishment – basic physiological needs that children rely on their parents to provide. Failure to do so would lead to children being taken into care.

### Capacity to adapt
The pace of social change makes the capacity of individuals to adapt to new realities increasingly important. The ability to learn and earn in constantly evolving landscapes is fundamental now to people's life chances. Evidence indicates that families have a more profound influence on children's ability to learn than schools; in fact parental involvement in learning has a significant effect on children's learning even after all other factors (social class, maternal education and poverty) have been taken out of the equation.[10]

## Emotional resilience

In his book *Emotional Intelligence*[11] Daniel Goleman argues that human competencies like self-awareness, self-discipline, persistence and empathy are more significant than IQ for people's life chances and that children can and should be taught these capabilities. Equally, feeling in control of life has a greater impact on happiness than many other factors. For example, workers who have more say over their working time feel less stressed and are more satisfied with and committed to their work; over two-fifths of full-time workers thought they would be more productive if they were given more control over their time.[12]

Family life has an impact on the emotional resilience of children. We know, for example, that incidences of depression are higher for children whose parents have no educational qualifications, or are on a low income.[13] And as another study has argued, 'There is consensus among investigators that warmth, regulation and respect for the child's autonomy are important parental characteristics in achieving optimal outcomes for children.'[14]

## Social exchange

In *The Support Economy*,[15] Shoshana Zuboff and Jim Maxmin argued that being an individual is fundamentally social. Although people are increasingly rejecting old-style group membership in favour of more diffuse communities of interest, this does not change the human interest in being connected and participating in relationships with others, whether that's about being a citizen, or a parent. At its most basic, people seek relationships that provide trust, love and support.

Families play a vital role in teaching us how to connect and enter into relationships with others. In 1904, Helen Bosanquet, social reformer and writer, declared that 'families are the nurseries of citizenship'.[16] And for many current parents, for all the professional support and guidance on offer from the wealth of books, TV programmes and parenting practitioners, they still cite their own parents as the major influences on how they parent themselves.

*I expect a man to do it all . . . because my dad did that.*
                                                               Father

*I do with my kids as my parents did with me.*
                                                               Mother

These basic family roles and responsibilities can be represented as shown in figure 1.

As we have outlined above, all the indicators suggest that the family – when compared with other factors and influences such as schooling, friends and wider society – plays a pivotal role in ensuring

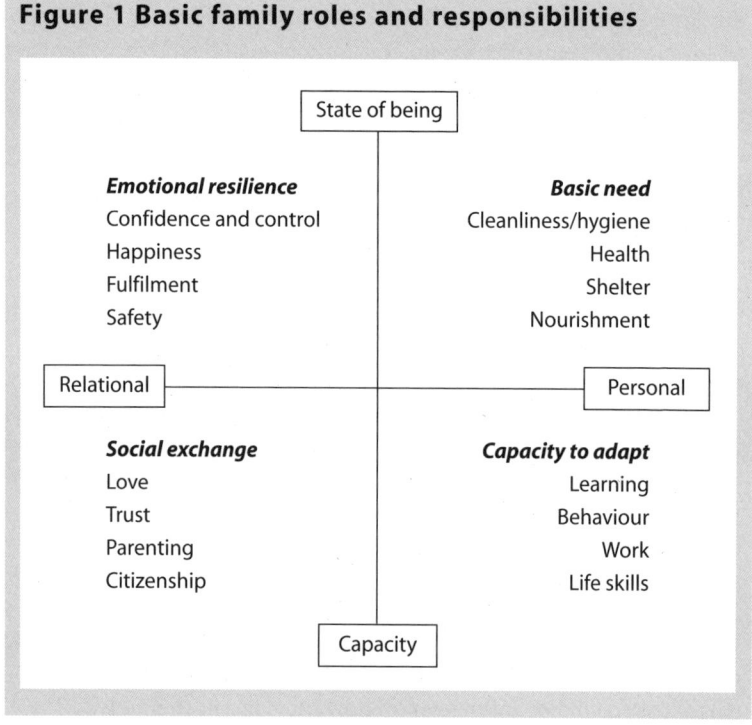

Figure 1 Basic family roles and responsibilities

children achieve these outcomes. So what are families for? One way of answering this question is to see them as groups of people working together to help individual children grow up into balanced, happy, adaptable and social adults.

This was emphasised by Alan Johnson, Secretary of State for Trade and Industry, in a speech in early October 2005:

> *Having a child is one of the most momentous events in life. We need to do more to help hardworking mothers and fathers balance their work and family commitments so that they can give their children the best possible start in life.*[17]

What is most notable about this model, however, is that although the elements of the model – basic need, capacity to adapt, emotional resilience and social exchange – all convey benefits to individual children, they are also shared goods with a public value. These goods can be both personal and immediate, such as the good health of a child, or collective and future-focused, such as the capacity to be a good parent or citizen.

## The public value of families

> *Perhaps the greatest social service that can be rendered by anybody in the country and mankind is to bring up a family.*
>
> George Bernard Shaw

Too often, the family is treated as a purely private sphere; the one place in our lives where we can retreat from interventions and impositions from others. But while privacy is a right that should be closely guarded, there is no escaping the fact that what families do is of public value, as well as benefiting family members as individuals.

Thinking about the 'basic need' segment of our diagram in figure 1 helps to illustrate this point. If families fail to provide basic needs for their children, then they will be taken into care. This has serious implications for the children in question, but also society at large. We know that looked-after children are vulnerable to missing out on education and have lower levels of attainment.[18] They are 13 times more likely to be excluded from school than their peers; young people who are excluded from school are more than twice as likely to report having committed a crime as young people in mainstream school.[19] Just 1 per cent of children who have grown up in care go on to university. This has a knock-on effect on the job market – a graduate is almost four times as likely to be in work and likely to earn twice as much as a person with no qualifications.[20]

Equally, considering the 'personal capacity' segment, there is a wealth of evidence to suggest that if parents do not help their children to develop the capacity to adapt and learn, there will be a significant impact on their educational outcomes. This can lead to children performing less well in their GCSEs – an effective pointer to whether they able to pass the capability threshold that qualifies them for the world of work at all, and for effective participation in society.[21]

Similarly, a number of longitudinal studies have found that two of the prime predictors for future offending are family poverty and poor parenting.[22] Anti-social behaviour in childhood is a better predictor than parental social class in understanding how much an individual will 'cost' society in adulthood.[23]

The concept of 'public value' has been much discussed in policy circles in recent years. Mark Moore, author of *Creating Public Value*, defines it as:

> *what the public values – what they are willing to make sacrifices of money and freedom to achieve.*[24]

There are four elements of public value that are important for our analysis.

First, public value offers a way of understanding families as adding up to more than the sum of their parts. Clearly every person within the family should be able to recognise the value of their efforts to create positive family settings for themselves; equally they should feel able to recognise the importance of belonging to a society which values families as crucial elements of the social fabric.

Second, public value frameworks attempt to capture the intangible as well as the measurable value of goods, taking account of the multiple activities and tasks of bringing up children. Despite the risks of woolliness or utopianism, 'public interest', 'public service' and other related concepts have tremendous symbolic power, and communicate something valuable, even if we can't define exactly what that value is. Bozeman has described this paradox as 'accruing not from the veracity of the argument, but from the difficulty in framing the argument'.[25] The point is, it is unlikely that we will ever be able to quantitatively *measure* the value of positive family life, but this should not mean that we refuse to believe it's important.

Third – and this is a theme to which we return in the concluding chapters of this pamphlet – public value cannot be created, in today's societies, simply by coercing behaviour through instrumental means, even if the intention is public-spirited. The challenge is to mobilise and motivate people to create that value themselves. In these terms the role of the state must be seen as enabling, removing barriers to public value creation and designing organisational innovations that enhance people's capacity to participate in the creation of value through bringing up their children.

Finally, public value drives a focus on how families themselves combine the various resources they have to hand to create that value. Mary Midgley[26] has written about the 'philosophical plumbing' of institutions, while Peter Hennessy[27] famously described the 'hidden wiring' of the constitutional state. Our argument is that if we want to understand more about how families can be supported in creating public value, we have to delve deeper into understanding how families are really working to create that value in the first place. With that in mind, the next chapter explores some of the ways in which families are currently organising themselves for the business of childrearing.

# 2. Getting behind the front door

## A typology of everyday family life

'Public value frameworks' and 'producing shared goods that are public' risk taking the family itself out of family life. To avoid this risk, we have conducted original research to understand the public value of families from the perspectives of families themselves. Starting with families, rather than frameworks, underlines the messiness of day-to-day life in most households. It's made up of getting the kids up and keeping them clean, feeding everyone, making sure there are washed clothes, filling lunch boxes, taking the rubbish out, keeping the car running, remembering birthdays, sorting out Christmas presents, mopping the floor, doing the shopping, and visiting grandparents and friends.

As growing numbers of families have two parents who are combining employment and unpaid care, the complexity of everyday family life is more pronounced than ever. Parents are expending tremendous energy on managing the dual demands of work and children; however, every family invents and adapts their own approaches to this juggling act. Arrangements are often precarious, a patchwork of support knitted together through almost constant reviewing and negotiation between parents, family, childcare providers, friends and employers.

There are as many families as there are ways to combine resources – economic, physical, social, spatial, personal and cultural – to look after their children and manage the dual challenges of employment and care. As part of our research to understand family life (see box below and appendic C for a description of our research process), we have developed a typology from a series of in-depth interviews and focus groups with families. This typology describes the many ways that families combine the full range of resources they have.

> **The research process**
> 
> This research project focused specifically on 'hard-working' families – in other words, families where both parents were likely to work, where they were not in crisis, and where they had at least one dependent child under the age of 12. Between February and March 2006 we spoke to a range of families from across the socio-economic spectrum, of different ages and stages in family life, from different ethnic backgrounds and in various states of employment. We asked each person to fill in a diary recording how they spent their time in the days leading up to the interview and used this as a starting point for the conversations. We spent time in their homes speaking to family members individually about the characteristics of their family, how they organised their daily activities and how they expected things to change in the future. We also worked with them to complete a series of activities and asked them to point out important objects in their home, to help us build up a picture of their family life.

We began by identifying pinch points in family life, or times that families found particularly stressful. These included when the first child was born; when a child had a contagious illness and standard forms of childcare broke down; when a child started school; when a second or subsequent child was born; and when parents took on additional caring responsibilities, for example looking after their own parents.

These pinch points helped to bring into sharp relief the delicate support structures that families build around themselves as part of day-to-day life and the ease with which it can all fall apart – when a child needs to be collected from school in the middle of the day or if the childminder is sick and parents are left in the lurch. Focusing on these stressful moments enabled us to concentrate on the values and assumptions on which each family's approach to managing employment and unpaid care were based.

This is an illustrative typology rather than a complete topography of modern family life. We have deliberately focused on 'hard-working families' made up of couples and dependent children as a means of unpacking the ways in which paid and unpaid work are negotiated and organised.

Despite not being a map of the full terrain, in the cast of British families, the characters in our seven family types are people who should be better understood. The typology is not about describing a hierarchy or identifying right ways, wrong ways or better ways of organising family life. Nor is it about fixing people into certain types – many of the families we spoke to moved through a number of the types we identified at different stages of their family life. Instead, it is about describing, analysing and understanding the ways in which families adapt to meet the dual challenges of paid work and childrearing.

## Typology of twenty-first-century households

The art of motherhood – *'Mum's the word'*

Frustrated feminists – *'If you can't beat them, join them'*

Domestic democracy – *'We've come a long way, baby'*

Everybody needs good neighbours – *'You want to go where everybody knows your name'*

Keep it in the family – *'The family that eats together, stays together'*

What money can buy – *'You can't buy love, but for everything else there's MasterCard'*

The survivors – *'Getting by matters more than getting on'*

## The art of motherhood

*A lot of my friends are a few years younger than me. They are a bit different. They don't cook for their husbands, they are not house-proud, a lot aren't married. They just iron when they need it. But I enjoy looking after my house, my children and my husband.*

Mother

There are lots of women who define themselves first and foremost as mums and housewives. Choosing to look after their families and homes is something that they are proud of and feel good about. If they have a partner, he contributes in a different way to the family with his role as breadwinner fitting into traditional expectations. But these families do not describe themselves as traditional – their defining feature is that the woman dominates the domestic environment and controls the reins of family life.

These women actively choose to define themselves as mothers. For some this is an easier decision than others, depending on what other opportunities are available to them. They may have found the jobs on offer to them as women with children drastically reduced, with those jobs that are available offering much less opportunity for stimulation, creativity and self-esteem than motherhood. But whether it's about creating an identity out of something that could have otherwise been quite negative, or actively choosing motherhood over a career, the identity of these women rests firmly in the home.

*Handing over your child to a stranger is not that appealing when there's not much for you at work.*

Mother

But most families find it hard to pay the bills on a single wage, so most of these mums work, many of them opting for caring professions such as childcare, teaching and nursing. Their jobs will be locally based, providing them with good networks of support with other mums. These jobs also explicitly value the skills that the women have developed as parents, and importantly they offer flexible working. Working around their child's school hours, or working as a childminder so that they can look after their own children at the same time, is crucial. These women take full responsibility for childcare, which means finding ways of looking after their children themselves.

*I made a conscious decision to work with children – you get the best of both worlds. . . . I wouldn't be a nursery nurse if I wasn't a mum.*

Mother

But none of these mums would call themselves a 'working mum'. Instead they would describe their work as a means to an end, with their salaries often being used to pay for family 'extras' including holidays, presents and eating out on special occasions. If they found themselves in a position where their wages were not covering the childcare bill the decision to leave the workplace would be clear-cut.

*I wasn't a working mother by choice and I don't see myself as that – a proper working mother would be high powered and have a nanny and a cleaner.*

Mother

Women remain in control of their domain. In many cases this means doing everything themselves, as their partners do not live up to their exacting standards. This control means the division of labour stays as it is; the woman's power-base is in the home and she is not prepared to relinquish it.

In these families the allocation of domestic tasks and childcare is based on the understanding that there are men's jobs and women's jobs. The man's domestic role is typically outdoors doing the gardening, DIY and driving with more occasional childcare responsibilities, while the women's role is focused on household organisation, chores and everyday childcare.

This allocation is a natural process that is rarely resisted or negotiated, and the division of activity is often in train before they have children. It is driven by an implicit but strict understanding of 'who is good at what'. For many women their partner's comparative ineptitude in domestic tasks is a point of amusement, and any tension is alleviated by appreciation and understanding of her workload. However, this soon breaks down if she is taken for granted or her work is not appreciated.

*I don't get as involved at home as my wife. . . . It's hard, I don't know how she copes.*

Father

If these families had a motto it would be: **'Mum's the Word.'**

### Frustrated feminists and doubtful dads

*We were both fantastically naive and thought we could do the lot. . . . At the time the big thing was for women to achieve what men can achieve. We've both abandoned proper careers but still work full time. . . . We haven't really sorted it out.*

Father

Frustrated feminists grew up believing that their path to success was to follow in men's footsteps in the workplace. They have dedicated a significant chunk of their life to their career, but as they have become mothers have realised that there just isn't enough time to have it all. Their partners have found themselves in a similar position – they grew up expecting that things would be simple with work and family life easily balanced, but reality has proved much more complicated.

These couples had their first child in their 40s – by the time they decided to start a family, they were probably older than they anticipated. But this isn't just about women. The decision to start a family is generally a collaborative one and there are a lot of doubtful dads out there and a growing number of men who are choosing their bachelor pad over a family home.

These families have struggled to find satisfactory ways to balance work and family life. On the one hand they are not able to dedicate as much time or head space as they would like at work, while on the other they feel that they are missing out on their children growing up. They tried to have the best of both worlds, but have ended up with an unhappy medium.

> *You're damned if you do and damned if you don't – there's no comfortable way to be a parent these days.*
> Father

They are likely to be graduates who moved away from home to go to university and have settled somewhere that is convenient for their job. Their friends are scattered and they do not have the support of their family close by. This set-up means that parents use a combination of formal childcare, whether it's nurseries and childminders or breakfast clubs and after-school activities.

> *My wife wanted children a few years ago, but I kept pushing it back. When she turned 40 I thought it would be unfair to leave it any longer.*
> Father

For the dads, the decision to delay fatherhood might be to do with 'the right time', but lack of confidence about what it means to embark on fatherhood and what it means for dad's identity may be a contributing factor, too. Some of these dads talk about choosing to spend more time at work over spending time with their families as they either lack motivation or confidence to be further involved.

> *I kept handing over control but it kept on coming back.*
> Mother

One way these families are responding to the challenge of integrating family life into a successful career is by setting up their own businesses, whether that's in childcare, marketing or consultancy.

> *I enjoy my work and look forward to getting up and out. It allows me to be me rather than just a housewife and full-time mum.*
>
> Mother

Frustrated feminists would not be happy if their identity was fully bound up in motherhood, and would never feel comfortable saying 'I'm a full-time mum'.

But being a 'career mum' hasn't worked for them either. Whether it's because of the attitude of their partner, their employer or that their values have changed, they have not been able to find a successful way of managing the allocation of parenting and working responsibilities.

If these families had a motto it would be: **'If you can't beat them, join them.'**

### Domestic democracy

These families are an unusual breed and they know it. They are self-conscious and considered and certainly wouldn't describe themselves as typical. They have found ways to balance the web of paid and unpaid work that makes up family life by challenging traditional divisions of labour in and out of the home.

> *I don't think we're a typical family, not the amount of stuff that he does round the house. . . . We're definitely unusual like that.*
>
> Mother

Both parents are probably in careers that they enjoy and do not want to sacrifice. They may well have chosen flexible jobs or sought out family-friendly corporations to make their aspirations a reality. These families are likely to count their employers as a main source of family support.

Their childcare arrangements are likely to be very complex – a jigsaw of nurseries, childminders, friends and family, flexible working and part-time nannies. Although nannies are expensive they offer the kind of flexibility than these families demand.

> *My husband deliberately doesn't work five days a week; he looks after our daughter on Wednesdays not because it's a duty, but because he really wants to.*
>
> Mother

With both parents working they are likely to miss out on most of the benefits designed for people less well off than them, so feel that they get a raw deal from the government. They may belong to groups of parents who share childcare, or join clubs focused around particular leisure activities and view these as alternative forms of support.

With both parents working one driver of negotiation will be time, or lack of it. But this isn't the only basis for their decision-making. Domestically democratic parents will share a strong set of family values; while they both want to work they also want to have an equal input into family life. This shared understanding is something that they look for and appreciate in each other.

> *We both want to be involved in family life and that's domestic tasks too. . . . We both want to do everything.*
>
> Father

They are explicit in their negotiation and the sharing of domestic tasks and responsibilities, and are expert in juggling household chores, with childcare, work commitments and socialising. They also share their parenting responsibilities equally, with dads in these families as likely to be involved in the emotional side of parenting – having private talks with children and helping with homework – as mums.

> *It's give and take, we support each other. . . . I've been through tough times and she stood by me. . . . We work together. I'm in charge of upstairs and she cleans downstairs, that's just how it works.*
>
> Father

## Getting behind the front door

Becoming a domestically democratic family is no mean feat and something that these families have worked long and hard to achieve. This kind of balance often arises after a crisis where families have been forced to challenge the way they do things or reassess their priorities. In many cases the mother will have been the driver of negotiation, challenging accepted roles and responsibilities.

> *When children came along our routines went up in smoke – now it's a rolling development, we get together and divide up the jobs as they arise. . . . We always talk about it, but she starts the conversations.*
>
> Father

The parents are likely to have a very honest and open relationship as they operate through a constant round of negotiation, dialogue and debate – this relationship between the parents may well be reflected in the family as a whole, with them discussing big decisions such as moving house or where to go on holiday with their children.

If these families had a motto it would be: **'We've come a long way, baby.'**

### Everybody needs good neighbours

> *We're very 'average average'. We work normal hours, she works part time locally and the children go to the local school and nursery. . . . I love everything here, it's all on our doorstep, that's really important, it's all on our doorstep.*
>
> Father

These families would describe themselves as 'very typical'. Both parents will characterise their work as jobs rather than careers. This isn't to say that work is not important, but that it is one factor in a range of elements that makes their family tick. They live their lives within narrow but comfortable horizons having little urge to break out beyond what they know.

> *I don't really like travelling, we don't go away much. Even going to Waterloo was scary, I thought I might get lost.*
>
> Mother

The parents are likely to have met locally and have a shared history or strong personal identity in the local area. This shared background will be an important source of strength in their relationship, and shape their values as a family.

> *We share values about childrearing; what they eat, how we want them to be educated, how they behave. . . . That comes from similar upbringings, which makes life easier.*
>
> Mother

These families will have a tight-knit network of extended family close by with whom they have lots of contact. They probably rely on their family for childcare, valuing the relationships that their children develop, as much as the practical and financial benefits of informal care. They may have even moved to be close to a set of parents, or never left the area in which they grew up.

> *I wouldn't leave my mum; I'd have no babysitter and no family ties.*
>
> Mother

However, these relationships go beyond practical support; their family and community are likely to be a main source of emotional support, a hub of knowledge and a source of learning.

> *I learnt everything from my mum – I lived at home with the first one so we just sort of did it together.*
>
> Mother

They describe their neighbourhood as a place where people look out for each other and would count the people who live close by as an important source of support, especially in an emergency. For single parents, people who have moved away from their family, or parents whose extended family live overseas this support is even more important. For some single parents their extended family and local community are a more consistent and trustworthy source of support than their partner or the child's dad.

> *My dad does night shifts so he can look after the little one – he's my saviour, I wouldn't be able to do it without him.*
> Mother

But, it's not just about having people nearby; it's about having everything nearby. These families are likely to shop and socialise locally. The mum might be part of a coffee morning or attend a local playgroup and the dad might belong to the local football or rugby club. They will try and send their children to local schools, within walking distance if possible, and will prioritise meeting them at the school gate.

> *On this road everyone's just like us, that's why we moved here.*
> Mother

So for these families, the boundaries between those who live in their household and those who are family are blurred – they see their family as part of a richer network of support and loving relationships. They are quick to talk about the help that they receive, but are as likely to be the providers of that support.

If these families had a motto it would be: **'You want to go where everybody knows your name.'**

### Keep it in the family

> *We don't get any support. . . . The rest of the family is a waste of time . . . you have to do it for yourself, especially when times are tough. Friends might be around but they don't stay around for long when you really need them.*
> Father

These families see themselves as an independent unit, with clear-cut boundaries around who's in and who's out. The way they organise their family life feels relatively straightforward, as they are echoing what their parents did. These families are traditional, with Mum as homemaker and Dad as breadwinner. They have not questioned the script of marriage, house and children; it just seems like a normal progression. But the fact that they are traditional is not their defining feature. It is their aggressive independence and the fact that they draw strength from their isolation that characterises these families.

> *It's how you were brought up isn't it? I do with my kids as my parents did with me.*
>
> Father

The dad will see it as his responsibility to provide for his family and it will be through this that he defines himself as a husband and a father. Mum probably does not work, perhaps feeling that it has a detrimental effect on family life – she will feel that her responsibility lies in the home. This isn't to say that these dads are not involved in family life, quite the opposite. These families will value the relationships within the family highly and will make a conscious effort to talk about issues as a family, and eat together in the evenings.

> *I think it's important to eat together, that's their way of talking to their dad, at the meal table.*
>
> Mother

These families probably stick to strict routines in terms of household activities and tasks. Rather than being negotiated, the division of labour will have developed naturally, based on their experiences of family life, and was probably in place before the couple had children. Although they are aware that other families do things differently, the parents do not see any need for new ideas or different ways of doing things. They fall back on tradition and familiar ideas as anchors in the face of change.

> *Household jobs are a woman's job. He's going to work full time, bringing in money – everything else is a bonus. . . . It's how my parents did it. A man doesn't need to come home to a house in a mess and no dinner.*
>
> Mother

Typically, these families are resistant to outside help – why should they do it differently from their parents who managed alone? This resistance is often characterised by a distrust of outsourcing any activities that are traditionally carried out in the home including cooking, cleaning and childcare. For single parents the issue of trust often goes deeper as they alone are responsible for maintaining their family unit.

> *It's worse for single people to find suitable childcare – it's hard to find people you trust.*
>
> Mother

If there is no alternative to both parents working, and they have to use some form of childcare, these families are likely to use informal childcare perhaps looking to their parents for some contribution. Alternatively the mum may have joined the growing number of mothers who, dissatisfied with the childcare options available, have chosen to set up their own childminding business at home.

The independence that distinguishes their family unit will be reflected in the strength of the relationships within the family. These families are likely to see issues that arise in society not as something that they are part of or have contributed to, but as issues that will disrupt family life. Their home is the place that they bring up their children – they will not see themselves as part of a community or wider social process and will see any attempt to support them in their role as parents as unwanted interference.

If these families had a motto it would be: **'The family that eats together stays together.'**

## What money can buy

*We have someone living in for the children, and a cleaner as it's impossible with the kind of jobs we've got. . . . It's given us our lives back. Now I can focus on work, enjoy time away and time together.*

Father

These families have found a way to balance work and family life at a price that most people can't afford – by outsourcing their childcare, cleaning and the day-to-day management of their family home. To have enough money to do this, both parents probably work full-time, although they might have taken the decision for one partner to stay home if they have enough money from one wage to live comfortably.

*As soon as we had surplus income we had choice for the first time. . . . My partner has chosen to stay at home as a full-time mum now – we decided that if we were going to have another baby we wanted to do it properly.*

Father

But this is not about straightforward consumerism; time is a commodity for these people as well. They feel a tension between committing time to their jobs and their caring responsibilities – this means that when they are at home they feel more tired, stressed and preoccupied. In other words, it is quality-time that suffers, and it is this that these families are trying to 'buy'.

Many of them are older parents who may well have imagined that they would have offspring in their 20s, but whose career, lifestyle or failure to find 'Mr or Miss Right' has meant that they are trying to juggle family life while reaching the pinnacle of their career. It is not that these parents are totally career driven or work focused, but that they aspire to and enjoy a certain life style that they are not willing to sacrifice. Working for the quality of life to which they have become accustomed, whether that's a bigger house, holidays abroad or quality time as a family or alone, is a priority.

## Getting behind the front door

> *My parents were shocked when I went back to work, as I didn't really have to but I'm used to certain standards. . . . I'd probably rather work part-time but it would be hard getting used to part-time money!*
>
> Mother

But, unlike the 'domestically democratic' families, these families are unlikely to count their employers as a source of support. In fact, for some the work place culture in their organisations has led them to buy in support rather than try to be flexible themselves.

> *My employer has family-friendly policies, but it's just lip service. The fact that I arranged to leave early to pick up my daughter from nursery was mentioned twice in my appraisals before we employed a live-in nanny.*
>
> Father

These families will almost certainly have a cleaner, which resolves the question of who is going to clean the cooker or vaccuum the lounge after a long day in the office. They may also have a live-in nanny or use private nurseries that offer a small ratio of adults to children and provide detailed daily feedback on the emotional and physical wellbeing of the child. Importantly, they also prioritise individual learning and development of each child within a structured environment, which fits in with the emphasis that these families place on education and experience.

> *She's getting more out of it than I could provide at home.*
>
> Mother

As MasterCard claims, 'there are some things that money can't buy', or in this context some things that people aren't prepared to outsource. Although these families buy their flexibility they see this as a way of buying quality time as a family not about outsourcing parenting.

If these families had a motto it would be: **'You can't buy love, but for everything else there's MasterCard.'**

## The survivors

> *My thinking is, as long as they've got food in their tummies, there's food in the cupboards and everything's clean and tidy then we're doing alright.*
>
> Mother

These families do whatever is necessary to care for and keep their family going. Their priority is ensuring that the bills are paid and there's food on the table. They find different ways of sharing the working and caring load to make this happen. For families where there are two parents both will be employed, but many of these families find themselves in jobs with few employment rights.

> *My first daughter was born at 22 weeks and was really poorly so had to spend 6 months in hospital . . . but I had to work for the first 6 weeks to get my maternity pay as I wasn't entitled yet.*
>
> Mother

For dads this focus on money often results in very little choice about their role in the family. Due to a myriad of factors including the pay gap, job segregation and the high cost of childcare, dad is the primary breadwinner.

> *I felt crap going to work when Paul was very little. My wife was exhausted and I knew the day ahead for her was going to be pretty dull, but I also knew I had to earn.*[28]

But he is unlikely to be the only breadwinner. These families find a combination of shift work that maximises the amount of hours that the parents can collectively contribute, with parents working a number of shifts between them, or one parent doing a number of jobs. It is not only children who are affected by this way of life.

Between working and childcare, shifts and sleep, parents often see very little of each other.

> We don't get to spend much time together. . . . We pass in the night.
>
> Mother

However, finding ways to pay the bills isn't as simple as working longer hours. For many low-income families a second wage is negated by the cost of childcare, which is typically £141 a week for nursery care for a child under two, rising to nearly £200 per week in London.

> There's no incentive to work if your wages go straight to the nursery.
>
> Mother

For lone parents the situation is even harder as they are caught between wanting to provide financially for their children and also wanting to be there for them. If they do go back to work they find ways to balance work and childcare by relying on a variety of family members, often grandparents, to help out.

> Childcare and affordable childcare is really important. The government is always saying go back to work. I feel as a mum that I want to be there for my kids but also you have to provide for them. Childcare is the most expensive thing – on a par with a mortgage.
>
> Mother

In these families, parents are likely to see their role hampered by a lack of money, with the mortgage and childcare being the biggest outgoings, although some will be eligible to claim back the majority of their childcare costs through the childcare element of the Working Tax Credit. However, many are either unaware of the support that is available to them, or just miss out on it.

These families point to lack of financial resources as the main barrier to their child not reaching his or her potential. This is not just about money per se; it is also about finding the time and energy to take part in sports or cultural activities even if they are free.

If these families had a motto it would be: *'Getting by matters more than getting on.'*

## Different folks, different strokes

This typology reflects the tenacity of family life in many different forms. Whatever way families choose to divide up the tasks that make up family life, it is busy, complicated and messy. Parents are expending vast amounts of energy, passion and determination in making their families work. And no matter how different these families are, they are all striving to create the best possible environment they can for their kids.

A common theme across all these family types is the interaction and relationship between paid work and unpaid work. Culturally, after 50 years of consumerism and growing individualism, we are placing greater emphasis on paid work than ever before. Yet unpaid care work is central to most families' experiences. How families navigate this tension is predictably influenced by a set of external drivers and trends that serve to limit the ways in which families are able to organise their resources in order to bring up their children and so create shared goods.

Families do not operate in isolation from the rest of society. What they do impacts on society and the decisions about how they do it are shaped by society. The rest of the report takes a look at patterns and trends in paid and unpaid work, drawing both on our own research as well as existing data. We explore how families view the relationship between paid and unpaid work, before considering the extent to which our seven family types really are free to make their own choices about the best way of using their resources to create public value.

# 3. Paid work
## What is productive?

*The norm in modern traditional families is for both parents to work, and to be working harder than ever before. This is not at the cost of their children, but at the cost of their own time and time with their partner. Men and women alike emphasise the equal importance of paid and unpaid work to family life, but this parity remains unrecognised by mainstream debate and policy formulation. A progressive politics for families needs to keep productivity in perspective by shining a light on the hidden value of the unpaid care that goes into raising future generations. This unpaid work deserves equal prominence to questions about making paid work better for parents in the debate about how to best support families.*

### The meaning of paid work for families

The massive growth in women and mothers entering the labour force is one of the most significant trends for the last 30 years. It means that for most modern traditional families, a dual income model has superseded the sole male breadwinner. Seventy per cent of couples with dependent children both work; 53 per cent of women with children under the age of five work, and 86 per cent of fathers work full time.[29]

Since 1997 the Labour government has introduced a raft of legislation to support working parents and help them get back into the workplace: the minimum wage, enhanced maternity provision, childcare and working family tax credits, higher child benefits and the New Deal for Lone Parents.

Once parents are in the workplace, they now have greater rights: the right to ask for flexible working if they have a child under six, the right to ask for unpaid parental leave for parents of children under five and unpaid time off to care for dependants, and the right to two weeks' paternity leave for fathers.[30] When the Work and Families Bill becomes law (expected in April 2007), women will have a right to nine months' paid and three months' unpaid maternity leave; men will have the right to three months' paternity leave at statutory rate provided the mother has returned to work; and the right to request flexible working arrangements will be extended to carers.

For many parents, these changes have been a welcome and important shift towards more family-friendly workplaces. But it has not led to the hoped-for 'win–win' situation where all parents believe they are able to combine employment with parenting successfully. There is some evidence that parents – particularly those who are highly educated[31] – are beginning to view family life as an obstacle to full participation in working life, rather than a life-changing and lifelong activity. This is borne out in particular for women, for whom motherhood reduces their earning potential. It is striking that while the majority of male chief executive officers have children, the majority of women in similar positions do not.

So there is an important contrast that needs to be drawn out, between the long, slow and linear extension of existing support to parents to enter (or re-enter) the labour force, and the degree of exhaustion, imbalance, stress and exposure that people are experiencing in seeking to *combine* work and childrearing.

In the stories that the families we spoke to told about their jobs, many parents were at pains to differentiate themselves from 'career women' or male breadwinners. Instead, paid work formed part of a much wider set of activities parents carried out to raise their children.

*He has a career, I just earn money.*

Mother

*I'm trying to cut down on hours and weighing up what you get out of it and what the kids get out of it.*
Father

People are not working because they 'want to have it all'; most are working because they have to. Nearly three-quarters of people working full-time want to spend more time with their families, and over a third of full-time and part-time workers are so exhausted when they get home, all they can do is fall asleep on the sofa in the evenings.[32] The idea that work buys cleaners and live-in nannies is only true for one in ten of the population.[33]

## Stacking shelves or lego bricks?

Current approaches to work–life balance issues are predicated on the assumption that getting people into paid work is always the best option for families. It is true that paid work is the fastest route out of poverty. However, it is also true that paid work for many people doesn't buy them choice; sometimes it doesn't get them much past poverty. Many families find that the difference between working and paying for childcare and not working at all is almost negligible. Women's work is still overwhelmingly concentrated in low-paid, low-status sectors: 75 per cent of working women have a job in one of the five lowest paid sectors and four in every five part-time workers, 80 per cent of whom are women, work below their potential.[34] So for many parents, particularly mothers, the idea of going out to work for the minimum wage, in order to pay for someone else to look after their children, makes little or no sense:

> *If aliens came down to earth and saw mothers paying other mothers to look after their children, they'd think we were mad.*
Mother

> *There's no incentive to work if your wages go straight to the nursery.*
Mother

Many of the families we spoke to expressed frustration about the lack of flexibility of available childcare.

*The nursery is good, but it doesn't fit in with my shifts. If I work 10am–1pm I have to pay for a morning and afternoon session – on those days I may as well not work.*

Mother

According to the Daycare Trust, there is currently one registered place for every nine children under eight.[35] The situation is worse in rural and disadvantaged areas: for example, in one single regeneration budget area, there was only one place per 27 children. Of the 6000 day nurseries in England, there are a mere 240 that are 'not for profit'.

Aside from being scarce, childcare is also expensive, despite government commitments to creating a free childcare place for every three- and four-year-old. Typically childcare costs £6000 for a family with two children, more than is spent on food or housing. According to the Daycare Trust's 2005 childcare costs survey,[36] the typical cost of a full-time nursery place for a child under two is £141 a week in England; that's over £7300 a year, a rise of nearly 5.2 per cent since 2003 – three and a quarter times the rate of inflation. The current average award through the childcare element of the Working Tax Credit is £51.21 a week. There is no extra help for parents with three or more children.

## Static flexibility

That flexibility can be static seems like a contradiction in terms. But for many of the families we met, that is exactly what it was. Families have constantly evolving needs and often parents have to shift between different patterns of work to respond to these needs. Furthermore, flexibility was still unable to solve the familiar everyday family problems. Part-time work is neither here nor there if a child has a contagious illness.

For men in particular, the promise of flexible working rights has not borne the fruits we might have hoped for. We know that currently

**Table 1. Who looks after your child if he or she is ill and has to miss a day from school or nursery?**

|  | Fathers (%) | Mothers (%) |
| --- | --- | --- |
| I would take time off work | 23 | 44 |
| Child's other parent would take time off work | 30 | 3 |
| I would, I do not work | 13 | 33 |
| Child's other parent would, they do not work | 16 | 1 |
| Other family member | 5 | 6 |
| Organised formal childcare | 2 | 1 |
| Friend or neighbour | 1 | 1 |
| Other | 4 | 2 |
| No answer | 2 | 5 |
| Don't know | 3 | 4 |

Source: GfK NOP polling

women feel in a stronger position to ask for flexible arrangements than men. Whereas 27 per cent of women are working flexibly, only 18 per cent of fathers are[37] and men are more likely to have their requests rejected by their employer (14 per cent of men compared with 10 per cent of women).[38] This flexibility is borne out in the realities of family life – in our polling, 44 per cent of mothers say that they would take time off if their child was ill; only 3 per cent said their partners would do so (although 23 per cent of men claim they would) (see table 1).[39]

This suggests that while the extension of support for parents to return to work is a positive step, as a route to ever greater equality it is also finite. A recent Joseph Rowntree Foundation report has claimed that in less than 18 years, the assumptions in place currently for ensuring that 'work pays' for lone parents will no longer stack up.[40]

The idea of flexible working is only one step towards a more equitable and integrated approach to combining employment and childrearing. For many parents, far from freeing them up to make the best possible choices about how to raise their children, current approaches to flexibility leave them teetering on the edge of extreme stress much of the time.

## Work intensification

For modern traditional families, it is now the norm that both parents work. Not only are parents more likely to work, they are now working harder than ever: working life has intensified. This trend is reflected in a number of ways.

First, mothers are not only more likely to enter the labour market now, they are also likely to enter (or return to it) sooner than ever before. Sixty-seven per cent of mothers in 2001 returned to work within one year of childbirth, compared with just 24 per cent in 1981. The greatest increase in the employment rate over the last ten years has been among mothers with children under four.[41]

Second, weekend working is a common feature of modern family life. Four in ten families with dependent children, in which at least one parent works, have a parent who regularly works at the weekend. In single-parent families, it is 28 per cent. Weekend working is predominantly associated with lower skills and self-employment. Between 71 per cent and 80 per cent of these (depending on job category) say they have no choice in the matter; it is a job requirement.[42]

There is also evidence of a link between working very long hours (over 48 hours a week) and working at the weekend – twice as many working parents who worked at the weekend worked over 48 hours per week than working parents who did not work weekends (27 per cent compared with 12 per cent).[43]

Third, a sense of overwork is prevailing. Nearly a third of workers now say that they have less time for their caring responsibilities than they would like (compared with 21 per cent in 1992).[44] Fifteen per cent of the total workforce are dissatisfied or very dissatisfied with their jobs, and 61 per cent want to work fewer hours (split by gender, this becomes 70 per cent of men and 52 per cent of women).

**Relative values?**

At the same time as people are working harder, as this report has already noted, parents are also spending longer on childrearing activities every day than ever before. So if people are working harder, *and* spending more time on childcare, what gives? In a Netmums survey, 75 per cent of mothers said that a 'lack of time for me' was a source of stress in family life[45] and when asked to name one thing they would do more of if they had the time, physical exercise (32 per cent of fathers and 30 per cent of mothers) and social life (13 per cent of mothers and fathers) were the most popular.[46] It seems that parents are investing less time in either themselves or their own relationships. Many of the families we spoke to were struck by how little time they spent together as a couple when we asked them to keep their diaries:

*Some weeks it's like we're only passing like ships in the night.*
Mother

*It's not your children who suffer, it's your relationship . . . you just become a pair of carers.*
Father

As parenting has become a more exclusive activity, so its cultural significance seems to be on the move. David Buckingham argues that as this process takes effect, 'quality time' becomes a kind of commodity' as our 'What money can buy' families have found.[47] This commodification of time and family activity is a further pattern worth noting. It represents one way of dealing with the simultaneous pressures of more work and a greater emphasis on childrearing for parents, which we look at in more detail in the next section.

## Overworking and outsourcing

Domestic service accounts for almost 10 per cent of the workforce, and cleaners, nannies and gardeners combined now exceed the numbers employed in accountancy, water and gas supply or the railways.[48] One in five families say that they employ someone to look after their children.[49] This outsourcing of the core role of modern families – childrearing – has been satirised in the *New Yorker*, for example, which carried a cartoon of an angry parent towering over their child shouting: 'Just wait until your nanny gets here.'[50]

Although nannies and home-based help are the preserve of the wealthy, as more families have two working parents, they are having to outsource at least elements of their weekly childcare routine. For many families juggling jobs and children, this is the only way that everything can be done within the limited time they have. The quality of this childcare is of huge importance to families:

> *We have a really nice childminder – in fact it can be hard to get my daughter out!*
>
> Mother

> *We're very satisfied with our childminder. . . . She definitely supports the family and I try to pick up tips from her!*
>
> Mother

> *We spent a long time looking for someone local and small. . . . She's really happy there.*
>
> Father

Recent policy has prioritised choice for families. Parents are offered subsidised childcare; there is a commitment to free childcare places for all children aged three and four. A host of organisations like the National Day Care Association are further extending the offer of much-needed childcare options. As the comments above indicate, for many families such childcare provides essential and valued support

Paid work

and opportunities for social interaction for children and parents alike.

However, quality is as important as expansion when it comes to childcare provision. Current fears about quality – compounded by well-publicised research that argues formal childcare slows or damages child development – mean that for many parents, such childcare arrangements are not the ideal or preferred option.

Every survey that looks at parental attitudes to and demand for childcare returns the finding that families prefer informal forms of care – from friends and neighbours to extended family – over the formal provision offered by childminders and nurseries. The next most popular options are forms of childcare that take place within the family home.[51] The demand for this type of childcare is reflected in the growth in salaries of nannies. In London nannies are now earning a record £28,181, outstripping the pay of newly qualified nurses and teachers.[52] These preferences for childcare in the home have had little influence on policy-makers, who continue to focus on expanding the number of childcare places on offer at nurseries, children's centres and childminders, rather than thinking about alternative forms, or how to improve the quality of existing childcare through training and further funding.

Meanwhile, employers are beginning to expand our options for outsourcing family life, taking them well beyond childcare. There has been a rapid expansion in the 'home life' market over the last few years. Many of these new services are being driven by employers keen to find new ways of keeping their staff focused on the work in hand. City firms will now sort out your drycleaning, house sale, holiday plans and plumbing issues. Organisations like Accor claim to 'satisfy the employer's need for greater efficiency, while showing greater responsibility to the needs of the employee'.[53]

Although these kinds of outsourcing options are often limited to the very well-off families, patterns across the rest of our lives reflect a similar theme. Families may eat a 'home-cooked' meal more often now than they did in 1961,[54] but these meals are often 'home-assembled' rather than cooked from scratch. As Arlie Russell

Hochschild has argued, there has been in shift in our personal symbols from production to consumption. In other words, the value of being a family now rests in eating the cake with your child on their birthday, rather than baking the cake.[55]

Is this outsourcing of family life being done in the best interests of children? Parental hesitation about many forms of childcare – and the battle to find arrangements that they are confident in – suggest that it is an option people take not out of choice but out of necessity. Employers offering support to families are less interested in the wellbeing of the children, and more interested in their own productivity.

Other families have decided that they cannot achieve the flexibility or quality of life for their children by combining paid work with outsourcing. A growing number of families are, in Albert Hirschmann's words, choosing 'exit as voice'.[56] This strategy is explored more in the next section.

## Doing it for themselves: exit as voice

For many people – the mothers in particular – that we spoke to, the options that are available in the workplace are simply not good enough and growing numbers are reaching the conclusion that they cannot achieve the kind of balance they seek between paid and unpaid work within organisations. Through challenging the categories of career woman or stay-at-home mums, women are finding their own ways of integrating work and life in order to meet their own needs and ambitions.

> *I was earning money for me, it was time outside the home but it fitted in at home.*
>
> Mother

Two patterns underline this search for integration. First, the expansion of jobs relating to childcare provision has led to a growth in the idea of mums as childcare professionals. Most childminders are women with young children of their own, enabling them to combine paid self-employment with staying at home.[57] Women are training for NVQs in childcare, having some kind of professional involvement in Sure Start or their child's nursery, and playing an active role in their child's school. For many women working at the place where their child is also being looked after resolves the tensions and demands of being a working mum; 97.5 per cent of the childcare workforce and 87 per cent of primary and nursery teachers are female.[58]

> *I shifted into being a childminder when I had a child, so that I could stay at home. I feel I made the choice to have a child, and I needed to be responsible to adjust my life so the child's needs were met properly. I'm still a childminder . . . it's very demanding but it's also satisfying because I can see both the mum and the child are thriving, secure and happy.*
> 
> Mother

Second, as this comment indicates, a growing number of women are opting for self-employment and run micro-businesses out of their homes. In a Joseph Rowntree Foundation study of families combining self-employment and family life, almost half the mothers interviewed (47 per cent) had chosen self-employment mainly for childcare reasons, compared with a small minority of fathers (6 per cent).[59] Although overall women are less likely than men to be in self-employment (6.5 per cent of all working-age women in employment are self-employed compared with 15 per cent of all working-age men in employment), the *rate* of female self-employment has more than doubled over the last 20 years. Women start up one-third of new businesses and own 13 per cent of all businesses – the majority of these women are aged over 35. Many have family commitments; just under half have children aged 16 or under and one-fifth have a child under the age of five.[60]

> *I don't want to be working for people for the rest of my life; I want to work for myself.*
> 
> Mother

### 'Hard-working' families?

In the 1970s, EF Schumacher wrote about the dangers of treating the planet's resources as infinite when in fact they are finite. He was uncomfortable with the unerring focus on growth, productivity and consumption, arguing that 'the GNP may rise rapidly: as measured by statisticians, but not as experienced by actual people, who find themselves oppressed by increasing frustration, alienation, insecurity and so on'.[61]

There is evidence that Schumacher's argument is ringing true for families in 2006. As the male breadwinner model has evolved into families characterised by dual income households, parents are facing a time squeeze that makes the challenge of combining productive and reproductive work ever greater. The parity parents accord to paid work and unpaid work is not reflected in the public debates about work–life balance, which still focus too heavily on employment and workplace reforms. While work will continue to be a vital part of most people's identities, failing to recognise the equal importance of bringing up the next generation will limit the extent to which it is possible to value and strengthen the capacity of families to raise children.

Creating the most appropriate support for hard-working families must rest at least in part on what they believe to be the best way of enhancing their children's outcomes, rather than a single-minded, but also myopic, focus on the goal of increasing participation in the labour market.

The domestic politics of parenting starts with the importance of this dual emphasis on employment and family life that we encountered during our research. Progressive approaches to family policy will need to right the balance of current debates by shining a light on the hidden value of the unpaid care that forms an essential part of everyday family life. It is this unpaid care, and its distribution between family members, that the next chapter focuses on.

# 4. Mum's the word
## The other glass ceiling

*Women continue to take greater responsibility than men for family and home life. Although gendered roles within the home are normalised by parents, they are in fact the product of a wider set of cultural, social and institutional patterns that individual families find impossible to overcome. These patterns thwart the desires of women, and increasingly men, to allocate family resources in a more negotiated and equitable way. The challenge remains to find ways of ensuring that it is children's outcomes and the public value created by family life that drive the distribution of family activity, rather than these entrenched gendered attitudes.*

The dual earner model is now so common that is feels part of a normal description of family life. In the last chapter we explored the place of paid work in the family and argued that there is currently a gap between how parents understand that place, and the way that government conceives of the relationship between paid work and parenting.

In arguing that families see paid work as an integral part of family life – rather than seeing parenthood as an obstacle to be surmounted in order to participate in the labour market – it is impossible to miss the gendered dynamics of both paid and unpaid work in family life. That is what this chapter looks at.

Women currently shoulder a disproportionate amount of the

burden for ensuring that their families are creating the public value discussed in chapter 1 of this pamphlet. They take greater responsibility for looking after children, managing the household, maintaining social networks of extended family or friends.

The significance of this – the other glass ceiling – risks being lost in the familiarity of the assertion. Noting that women still do the double shift is almost a truism. Yet what it represents is no less significant than the barriers to advancement women continue to experience in the workplace.

Talking to families underlines the *dynamic interchange* between the resistant social and cultural realities of gendered labour patterns and the allocation of unpaid labour in the home. This chapter explores this in greater depth. Our research indicates that families themselves are increasingly aware of how gender politics are limiting the scope of choices they can make in bringing up their families; but this awareness has proved almost impossible to translate into action when faced with the systemic nature of gender inequality.

## How high is the ceiling?

Survey after survey has confirmed the existence of the glass ceiling in the home. The most recent Time Use survey published by the Equal Opportunities Commission shows that on weekdays mothers spend three times as much time on everyday household tasks as fathers, and twice as much time at the weekend.[62] Women are over 3.5 times as likely as men to say they did the majority of household tasks, and over 12 times as likely to strongly agree they do most of the childcare.[63] Men, if they do help with the family, are more likely to get involved in activities that are more occasional and focused on achieving a specific goal, for example, gardening, car-cleaning or DIY – 49 per cent of men spend at least two hours a week doing DIY, compared with just 25 per cent of women.[64] Women on the other hand reported that they were more likely to manage the everyday activities such as bathing children, vaccuuming, cooking and washing.

This distribution of chores seems to be set from childhood. Data collected for NOP Family and the Equal Opportunities Commission

**Table 2. Other than learning at school, which of the following do you consider as learning with your child?**

|  | Fathers (%) | Mothers (%) |
|---|---|---|
| Watching TV together | 44 | 39 |
| Reading together | 76 | 76 |
| Shopping | 26 | 32 |
| Playing sport | 56 | 39 |
| Cooking and other home activities | 48 | 68 |
| Visiting friends and family | 44 | 43 |
| Other | 2 | 4 |
| None | 3 | 7 |
| Don't Know | 2 | 2 |

Source: GfK NOP polling

shows that the chores that young people do in the home are already clearly gendered and reflect the tasks that men and women complete in the home. Girls do chores more regularly than boys and where boys do help out they only scored higher than girls in mowing the lawn and gardening, cleaning the car and DIY.[65]

> *My partner does help; I think he's exceptional. But of course there are some things he doesn't do; he won't do cooking, washing and ironing.*
> Mother

> *I'm happy with how we do things here; it's how it's been since we were married – he's happy to take the rubbish out and I don't want to.*
> Mother

This gender difference is reflected in the attitudes of mums and dads towards learning. According to polling carried out as part of this project by GfK NOP, men are much more likely to regard playing sport with their child as a learning activity compared with women (56% of men compared with 39% of women). Conversely, women are more likely to regard cooking and home activities with their child as a form of learning (68% of women compared with only 48% of men) (see table 2).

## Attitudes are as important as activities

The glass ceiling at home is as much about attitudes as it is about activities and how they are allocated. Even where parents proudly share all unpaid work activities absolutely equally (one family we met had divided their house in half and each partner took responsibility for everything in their half), family life across Britain is still shaped by a sense that women are the ones holding everything together. Women are taking a proactive role in creating the family that goes far deeper than allocation of activities.

> *I just do what I need to as I go along.*
>
> Mother

> *I don't not do it.*
>
> Father

> *I'm a willing but passive participant . . . I just don't look forward and see the challenges in the same way, but that doesn't mean I'm not interested.*
>
> Father

> *I feel the whole weight of the family rests on my shoulders, even though my partner does a lot.*
>
> Mother

In particular this difference in mindset is reflected by the fact that women carry almost all of the responsibility for maintaining the links between the family and the wider world. Women buy the birthday cards and presents. They visit the school and develop relationships with other mums in the local area. They shop for clothes for their children and know when it's time for new shoes. They find the babysitter and they make the shopping list, even if they don't actually do the shopping.

For some women, the attitude of their partners is at the heart of the continued existence of the glass ceiling at home.

> *I prefer to stay at work till 6; if I get in earlier I'd need to help with the kids. I feel like I've already done a whole day's work and I don't fancy starting again.*
>
> Father

> *His idea was that the woman looked after the children and he had a brilliant social life!*
>
> Mother

> *He has no idea about cooking, if I'm out at teatime the kids won't have been fed.*
>
> Mother

> *The assumption is that it's the woman's fault if the house is untidy, even when I don't create the mess. . . . I've tried to rebel against that but I've just ended up picking everything up.*
>
> Mother

These men are likely to be among the 20 per cent of men agreeing or strongly agreeing that the husband should earn, and the wife should stay at home.[66] But male attitudes alone are not enough to explain why, despite huge changes in working patterns and broader cultural shifts around equality and women's rights, the modern family model is still based on some very gender-specific roles which locate most women's identities primarily in the home and family.

## Boys will be boys and girls will be girls

Given the mainstreaming of feminism and equality debates since the introduction of sex discrimination legislation, there is surprisingly little anger or resentment about the glass ceiling in the home. Men and women alike argue that their household arrangements are the product of a set of individual choices and natural gender differences rather than any broader societal patterns of discrimination and gender stereotyping. There is a pragmatism to family life and gender roles: a sense that life's complicated enough without fighting about whose turn it is to change a light bulb.

> *There are boy and girl jobs – that's just the way it is.*
>
> Mother

> *We didn't mean to become stereotypical.*
>
> Mother

The majority of people, men and women, are 'literate' in sex discrimination in the workplace. There is a consensus that women should have equal rights at work, and that if a woman is not promoted appropriately or treated respectfully this is the effect of sexist attitudes and discrimination. Yet debates about equality, sexism and discrimination stop as the front door closes. Once at home, gender differences suddenly become the product of intrinsic or 'natural' gender roles. The fact that, despite working more, women continue to take responsibility for family life is not described in terms of inequality.

> *Household jobs are a woman's job. He's going to work, working full-time, bringing in money – everything else is a bonus.*
>
> Mother

> *Men can look after kids – but women do it better.*
>
> Father

Women – like our 'art of motherhood' family type – are as likely as men to share these views. Rather than raging against discrimination or fighting for a more equal distribution of responsibility in the family, women are quite playful about men and their ineptitude around the house. So when he tidies, he just flings everything in the cupboard, when he tries to cook she ends up sorting out the mess, when he does the washing he forgets to separate out the whites and the colours. The idea of men organising birthday parties, remembering anniversaries or knowing what the store cupboard basics are was met with gentle teasing in our research.

> *I just do everything myself because he doesn't do it properly, and I have to do it all over again. You just end up going round in circles.*
> 
> Mother

These kinds of attitudes reflect the complexity of women's feelings about their identity and their family. Many women simultaneously feel frustrated by the lack of support from their partners, and quite possessive of the family space as a site of agency and personal identity.

> *I find myself trying to control everybody's lives. . . . I'm a bit of a worrier.*
> 
> Mother

> *I'm there and I'm in touch. . . . I'm a well-known figure around the school.*
> 
> Mother

> *I'm a bit of a control freak – there was a time when I had to step back – and he had to step in – you can allow somebody else not to come in.*
> 
> Mother

## The art of negotiation

Despite these seemingly entrenched attitudes and values around mother and fatherhood, it was clear from our research that parents did not always feel comfortable with the distribution of domestic tasks. Women were often nervous when they realised it looked like they were doing it all.

*It looks so sexist but we don't live a sexist life, it's just easier like that.*

Mother

*When you're in a relationship and you're working together it's ok but if it's one-sided it's really hard. If you're sharing its much better.*

Father

And men were defensive about the arrangements in their households. They were keen to underline their willingness to contribute to the family in other ways, and their aspiration to take on more of the burden.

*We did think about me staying at home but we never really firmed it up.*

Father

*I would love to stay at home and look after my daughter, but we couldn't live on my wife's wage.*

Father

But in the families where this discomfort had led to explicit negotiation as an attempt to find a way to distribute paid and unpaid work, they faced social, cultural and institutional barriers to sharing the caring load.

*The people who are bending over backwards to make it work aren't the employers, it's the parents.*

Father

**A quiet revolution?**
The work–life balance debate has in part struggled to evolve due to

some of the gendered assumptions that underpin it. These assumptions serve to maintain the divide between family roles of both men and women. First, by saying 'parents' and meaning 'mothers'; and second, by assuming that the only people who are trapped are those who are stuck at home and not in paid work. Yet men and women alike talked about the levels of stress associated with being the main or sole breadwinner in the family.

> *When I lost my job and my partner was pregnant, I felt really stressed; I felt more vulnerable because I felt it was my role to look after and support my family.*
>
> Father

> *I became the breadwinner for a while . . . it was horrendous, very stressful just thinking about money all the time.*
>
> Mother

Without wishing to undermine the very real and serious gender discrimination that women still experience, a vital part of finding new ways of seeing debates about family life is to look afresh at fathers and fatherhood. There is a 'quiet revolution' among men. Fathers – particularly younger men – are expressing a greater aspiration to be more involved in family life. Equal Opportunities Commission research suggests that eight of ten fathers want to spend more time with their children. Many men, as well as women, report a desire to work less, and express regret about not seeing enough of their family. Ten per cent of the male workforce (compared with 19 per cent of the female workforce) have requested flexible working practices in the last two years – a massive increase on previous figures.[67] We heard comments from mothers and fathers to support these findings:

> *I quit my job because I wouldn't have a family life – and that's more important.*
>
> Father

> *He takes Wednesday off – not because he has to but because he wants to look after our daughter as well.*
>
> Mother

Gender equality cannot mean gender equality only in public life. As this report argues, public and private lives are inextricably linked at the level of the family and on this basis there has to be a renewed search for how to create greater gender equality in the private sphere of the family.

However, this is not about finding a universal solution to inequality; nor is it necessarily about finding new ways of enabling women to behave more like the traditional male breadwinner whose identity is heavily vested in his working life. As the last chapter indicated, families are beginning to question the desirability of this model.

Instead, the focus needs to be on understanding, and tackling, the factors that serve to constrain families from making what they feel are the best possible decisions for their children's life chances. All too often men reported that attitudes to men in work mitigated against their ability to turn their aspirations to be more engaged parents into action:

> *Employers don't care and don't understand – they're just interested in hitting targets.*
>
> Father

> *They just play lip service to family life; they don't really care as long as they get 20 hours a day out of you.*
>
> Father

That said, even with the most flexible employment practices and understanding employers possible, the odds of fathers taking on an equal share of the unpaid workload are still stacked against them. Many fathers express concerns about 'getting it wrong'. Parenting classes and services are designed overwhelmingly on the basis of the mother being the primary carer.

*He thinks he can't do something. . . . He does lack confidence about being a good dad.*
Mother

So there remains a lonely quality to many active fathers' experiences. This is hardly surprising – there are less than 200,000 stay-at-home dads in the UK and although this figure is rising it is not doing so exponentially. Fathers report feelings of exclusion, of 'being treated as an outsider' by schools, coffee groups and parent support services.

In all of the families that we spoke to there was a real sense that the distribution of the unpaid workload was up for debate, but for many this was *aspirational* and not played out in their behaviour. A significant contributing factor to prevent aspirations translating into action remains the gendered nature of participation in the labour market.

### Gender politics: the interaction between paid and unpaid work

Despite the tendency of parents to normalise their own experiences and see the division of gender roles as natural, there are some familiar social, cultural and institutional factors that serve to constrain the extent to which families can genuinely 'choose' how best to share the organisation of family life. These factors, which have been written about in greater depth elsewhere, make it easy to default to a 'modern traditional' family in its many forms.

### Discrimination at work

While more women are working, and working longer hours, they are still losing out in the workplace in a number of ways. Women are far more likely to work part-time than men; 80 per cent of part-time workers are women, and 80 per cent of them are working below their potential. Women's work is also lower paid. The pay gap for part-time women when compared with full-time men is 38.5 per cent, and 27 per cent when compared with a full-time woman. This has hardly gone down since 1975 when the gap was 41.6 per cent. The pay gap for full-time women when compared with full-time men remains stubbornly at 18 per cent, having risen slightly in the last four years. Women's median weekly income in 2002/03 was £154 compared with men whose weekly income was £288.[68]

Women are also less likely to be found in the boardroom making up just 8.3 per cent of top judges, 18 per cent of MPs, 30.5 per cent of secondary school heads, 12.4 per cent of local authority chief executives. While there has been an increase in the number of FTSE 100 companies with women directors to 78, only 11 of those have female board members holding executive positions and 22 of the top FTSE 100 companies have no women on their boards at all.[69] A depressing 30,000 women a year still lose their jobs because they are pregnant, and half of all pregnant women will experience some form of discrimination. Women returning to work after starting a family are around 40 per cent less likely than the average white, able-bodied man to be offered a post.[70]

**Skills deficit**

Focusing on the pay gap often obscures an equally significant pattern in paid work. 'Jobs for the boys and jobs for the girls' remains a powerful description of the labour market. Women are found overwhelmingly in five areas – cleaning, catering, care work, clerical jobs and check-out workers. Four-fifths of skilled tradespeople and machine operators are male and four-fifths of administrative and secretarial staff are female. This is a pattern that is likely to continue given that of the people studying for Modern Apprenticeships women comprise 97.5 per cent of those in early years and education, and 87.7 per cent in health and social care, compared with 0.6 per cent of those studying plumbing at this level. The greater the number of women participating in a sector, the lower the pay.

Women often go into jobs that traditionally offer flexibility whether in shiftwork, part-time or term-time working: 88 per cent of nurses, care assistants and home carers; 80 per cent of cleaners and domestics; and 77 per cent of retail cashiers and check-out staff are women.[71]

### Inflexible employment practices

Although there are undoubtedly more flexible working options in some sectors than there have been, flexibility still varies by levels of seniority and sector. Despite pockets of excellent or promising practice, the wider story remains centred on the ongoing inflexibility of employment practices overall.

This rigidity makes it especially hard for men to be at home: 95 per cent of firms provide bereavement leave, but just 65 per cent offer paternity leave.[72] While two in three companies currently offer paid paternity leave, the average length of leave taken is around three days. From April 2003 fathers were entitled to two weeks' paternity leave paid at the Statutory Maternity rate of £100 a week. However, initial monitoring of the new provision suggests that rates of uptake are lower than expected: only 19 per cent of new fathers took statutory paid paternity leave in the first year after the entitlement was introduced.[73]

When men want to make longer-term changes to their working practices, they are more likely than women to be rejected – one in seven men compared with one in ten women have their application for flexible working rejected completely by their employer.[74] We begrudgingly let Ruth Kelly clock off at 6pm and leave for home without the ministerial red box, but the fact remains that if a male minister did this it would still be complete anathema. The day we celebrate a woman – let alone a man – opting to work flexibly is still a long way off.

### Children's needs versus gender politics

All of these factors mean that when it comes to making choices about who does what in family life, more often than not women will end up taking a disproportionate amount of responsibility, while men will struggle to shift out of a pattern of full-time work towards a more integrated approach to family and career.

That factors like these, rather than necessarily what's best for children, are driving the ways in which families organise paid and unpaid work should be a cause for concern. Families that operate in the children's interests are also operating in the interests of society as a whole.

The question is how can families be better supported in co-producing the public value they create? And how can families themselves – rather than existing legacies of inequality and culture – determine how to allocate their resources to maximum effect? Far from endorsing a single family type that is seen to be 'better' at childrearing than other formations, these questions demand a renewed focus on how support can be designed that deals with a range – and indeed proliferation – of working family arrangements.

# 5. Public value, private responsibility?

*We are expecting families to bring up their children with less and less support, informal and formal, from civil society and the state. At the same time parents are feeling under greater pressure to be perfect parents. This has led to a stalemate: parents are stressed and lonely; the state is wary of intervening in the subtle dynamics of family life. Yet there are gains to be won for family, state and civil society if the relationships between these elements of the social fabric are strengthened. The challenge rests in casting the relationship in such a way that privacy is respected, but not at the expense of the best possible approach to maximising children's outcomes.*

How families organise themselves to bring up their children is of critical importance. It not only has an impact on the individual life chances of each of those children, but also on society more generally. Families are the sites of children's first lessons in negotiation, rights and responsibilities. So, far from being a 'haven in a heartless world',[75] families are vital sites of production – where the value they are seeking to create relates to the 'good society' as well as to those individuals within the family.

What is clear from the typology outlined in chapter 2 is that the vast majority of families are working hard to organise themselves in order to give their children the best possible start in life. But they are doing so in a context where the choices people feel able to make are frequently constrained by a host of factors that lie beyond the immediate locus of the family.

These systemic and institutional factors matter. They have a powerful influence on the extent to which families can organise themselves to genuinely meet the needs of their children. The last two chapters have focused on two of the factors that limit the degree of freedom families feel they have in creating public value: first, the conceptualisation of 'support' in the context of a hierarchy of activity where paid work is at the pinnacle; and, second, the gender dynamics at play in the interaction between paid and unpaid work.

In this chapter, we argue that there is a third layer of complexity that prevents families from necessarily being able to bring up their children in order to maximise their life chances. This is the increasing isolation and segregation of family life. It is played out both in how families relate informally to the communities in which they live, and in how the state currently casts its relationship to families.

## Decline in trust and social bonds

> *Nobody has ever before asked the nuclear family to live all by itself in a box the way we do. With no relatives, no support, we've put it in an impossible situation.*
>
> Margaret Mead[76]

Families are working to create shared goods in the context of increasing isolation and lack of surrounding support. Despite being a relatively content and affluent society, the signs are that mutual support and neighbourliness have declined in the UK. Longer working hours and greater mobility have no doubt contributed to this decline, demonstrated by the fact that a mere 29 per cent of the population believe now that other people could generally 'be trusted'. In the late 1950s this figure stood at 60 per cent; even at the start of the 1980s, it was at 44 per cent.[77] Another Demos report looking at informal social bonds on mixed-tenure estates found that only 15 per cent of respondents got to know fellow residents at local shops, and just 7 per cent did so at the local pub. Even the primary school, often seen as the institution that holds together many social bonds, succeeded in introducing only a third of parents to each other.[78]

The transformation of women's lives over the last 50 years, compounded by increased geographic mobility, has also had a profound impact on the nature of the informal support families have to draw on in producing these shared goods. In the 1950s, Peter Townsend calculated that three out of five older people in Bethnal Green belonged to 'three-generational extended families' – either by living with children and grandchildren, or by seeing them every day. Three decades later, the British Social Attitudes survey of 1998 found a mere 2 per cent of grandparents living in such households.[79] While our 'everybody needs good neighbours' families place huge emphasis on the importance of locally based networks of extended families, this is not the general spatial and geographic trend in modern British family life.

### Segregation of families and non-families

This decline in informal support has been accompanied by a wider cultural shift in how we see families and, in particular, other people's children.[80] Families are becoming not only more specialised – they are focused far more on childrearing than they were – but also more segregated from wider society. As Mary Crowley, chief executive of the Parenting Education and Support Forum said, 'for most women today, the first baby they hold is their own'.[81]

We don't like the children of our acquaintances: 57 per cent of us called them 'attention seeking' and 54 per cent of us called them 'spoilt'.[82] Public spaces and shared places are not designed to accommodate those with and without children together. Fears of paedophilia and of 'yobs' lacking respect have driven the creation of zoned spaces into which children are shunted, in the interests of either safety or containment. Housing developments – particularly in urban areas – focus on either family accommodation or on apartments for young affluent individuals or child-free couples. Attitudes to children in public spaces can be summed up by this comment, made by a restaurant owner:

# The Other Glass Ceiling

> *Children are very welcome as long as they do not cry or shout and if any other customers complain they will have to be removed.*[83]

This is an example of a wider sense that it is socially acceptable to reject families from public spaces or at the very least to segregate those with children from others without them.

As we argued in chapter 1, one of the results of this separation between families and wider society is that families feel that they are more responsible than ever for creating positive family environments by themselves, in the absence of supportive networks and state interventions.

## Paranoid parents

The weight of responsibility for producing public goods rests too heavily with families, rather than wider society. Parents are feeling under greater pressure to bring up their children 'in the right way' at the same time as feeling more alone. For example, 42 per cent of parents now report feeling responsible for ensuring that their child succeeds – five times as many as those who saw their child's success or failure as being the result of an unfair society.[84] People are worried about 'getting it wrong' in the context of ever more 'evidence' about what constitutes perfect parenting:

> *No one teaches you how to look after a baby, just basic stuff about how to change a nappy and make milk formula. For some people this just sort of comes naturally, but for others it couldn't be further from the truth.*
>
> Mother

> *All this health stuff – like Jamie's Dinners – is stressful . . . I want to do my best for the boys; I've bought his book so I know what to cook.*
>
> Father

The levels of concern that people report about their family life are far higher than their concerns about the health service or crime in their local area. Children's spare time is now more likely to be spent in the home watching television or playing video games, as parents feel that keeping their kids inside the house, supervised, keeps them safe. In one survey, 66 per cent of parents agreed that children spend too much time at home because of safety issues.[85]

So families are retreating into themselves. There are strong indications that parents specifically have begun to feel the pressure of creating successful families in the context of declining informal support and growing isolation. It is estimated that 16 per cent of parents have mental health problems.[86] The number of people feeling lonely has risen sharply in recent years: nearly half of all calls by parents to Parentline Plus cite isolation and loneliness as 'key concerns'.[87] According to Young Minds, these feelings are two of the most significant factors in making parenting difficult.[88] The figures for parents suffering from mental health problems can effectively be doubled (or more) as their conditions affect family members too.[89]

Specifically, levels of postnatal depression have been growing in recent years. In a survey conducted by Netmums, 52 per cent of mothers said they have suffered or feel that they may have suffered postnatal depression, whether it was diagnosed or not. The results for diagnosed postnatal depression were considerably lower at 27 per cent but even this is a significant rise from figures for the 1970s, which show that 11 per cent of mums were diagnosed.[90] Forty-two per cent of mothers felt that loneliness and boredom was one of the key factors that affected them.

## The state and families

It was 100 years ago, during the radical New Liberal administration of 1906, that the state tentatively began to impose on family life. The aftermath of the Boer War revealed a shockingly high proportion of the population was living in real poverty. A growing school of thought argued that this poverty was less an individual, moral or familial issue, and more a burden on and cost to society. In these terms, groups like the National Efficiency Movement, and thinkers such as JA Hobson, Sidney and Beatrice Webb and Joseph Rowntree, argued that the state had a responsibility and indeed a degree of self-interest in taking measures to alleviate the abject conditions in which large numbers of the population were living.

It was during this administration that the state began to reach into the heart of family life. Compulsory vaccinations, dental inspections and free school meals were introduced as measures that reflected the importance to society of healthy children, and the acknowledgement that some families were unable to create the shared good of future generations unaided.

Since this time, the state and families have had a complex relationship. At various points in the last 100 years politicians have attempted to regulate families and halt the perceived move away from solid, secure family units made up of children and two parents bound together through marriage. These have rarely been successful. Marie Stopes campaigned on birth control in the hope that the working class would be encouraged to limit the number of children they had, but instead family planning became the preserve of the middle classes. John Major's 'back to basics' campaign was met with glee by journalists, who used it to expose how *untypical* most cabinet members' families were. It seems that families have a predictable habit of doing things their way, whatever the politicians say.

More recently, moral exhortations about families have become less acceptable. Families have been held up as the ultimate private sphere, the one part of people's lives where interventions are not welcome. Politicians fear being accused of meddling, of creating an overbearing state where people cannot escape interventions even in the comfort of their own homes.

This nervousness about intervening in the private and sacred sphere, combined with the belief that parents are solely responsible for their children's outcomes, has driven a particular approach by this government. It is an approach where a family needs to be in real crisis before the state is able to intervene legitimately. The tragic death of Victoria Climbié demonstrates how bad things have to get before

## Public value, private responsibility?

state interventions put children's welfare before the parents' right to privacy.

This question – about the point at which the rights of children supersede the rights of parents to a family life – is one that needs to dominate debates about families and public value in coming years. It is a complex and controversial set of issues, beset by inconsistencies in both the legal framework of children's rights, and in the professional mores of people working with families across different public services.[91] It is not an issue we can tackle with sufficient depth in this pamphlet.

For now what is important to note is the fact that the state appears in many cases to be more nervous of intervening in family life than the families themselves are. The introduction of parenting classes for families where the child has been issued an Anti-Social Behaviour Order was controversial. Yet many parents who have attended these classes simply express relief – and regret that it took some kind of 'crisis' to trigger the support for which they had been asking for a number of years.

Recent research by the Equal Opportunities Commission indicates that families themselves expect the state to play a role in supporting family life. Respondents suggested that politicians talking about family issues stood a good chance of winning more votes, and people consistently report higher concerns about their family life than they do about the state of local health services or crime figures. Perceptions that the state and politicians are not interested in supporting family life cause anger, frustration and resentment:

> *There's no financial reason to stay together as a family, you're better off as a single mum [the benefits system] encourages people to split up.*
> 
> Mother

> *They don't encourage you to be a family at all, they punish you for it.*
> 
> Mother

People see their families as vitally important parts of their lives. They expect this to be recognised in political discourse; but they also expect to be respected as experts in childrearing and their own family's needs.

It is right that government is wary when it comes to attempts to shape the subtle dynamics that make up everyday family life. But this is not the same as ruling out any relationship between state and family at all. As we have argued in this pamphlet, families can be characterised as groups of people working together to produce shared or public goods. As such, there is a collective interest in what goes on in families that legitimates and indeed necessitates some kind of relationship between state, civil society and families.

Chapter 1 explored this argument in more detail. The point is that parents cannot always know what is best for children – not only their own, but other people's – nor can they necessarily tackle the demands of family life alone. The range of external factors that determine family decisions about the allocation of labour indicates that, at the very least, there is a role for the state in working with parents to ameliorate some of the constraints imposed by these factors on decisions about how to balance work and home life. The place of the state is less about moralising around family structures, and far more about how we can genuinely value and recognise the importance of what families do for all of us.

In the final chapter, we take the arguments of this pamphlet and begin to make some recommendations about the future direction we believe the work–life balance debate needs to take. These recommendations consider how support can be designed for *all* families, whatever their 'type', as producers of public goods. We consider how such support can be focused on building childrearing capacity, through helping families to make their own decisions – rather than external factors driving these choices – about how they go about producing these goods.

# 6. Opening up the scripts of family life
## Recommendations

This report has told the story of everyday family life, and has made the case for understanding families through the lens of 'public value'. What families do matters, not only to the children growing up in them, but to everyone. Bringing up the future generation is as important as being a productive citizen. Finding ways of recognising the value created within families, and supporting and enhancing it, is the focus of these recommendations.

At the heart of the approach proposed here is the recognition that helping families is a complex challenge. Our focus is on removing barriers, opening out family scripts and asking what's the best way of creating this public value. How can families be supported to use the emotional, physical, economic, social and cultural resources they have to maximum effect? How can the everyday activities of family life be combined and shared out in such a way that every family is creating the optimal conditions for the co-production of the public goods described above? How can we ensure that the distribution of resources within families does not place undue stress on particular family members?

The following recommendations focus on beginning to answer some of these questions, and in doing so offer an alternative vision of the relationship between families, civil society and the state – a vision that is grounded in the views and attitudes of families, but one that places the public interest in maximising children's outcomes at the forefront of the public policy agenda around families.

As we emphasised at the start of this pamphlet, our focus has been on the 'hard-working' families targeted by current government ministers, rather than those families in crisis. What we know from our research is that family life is an intricate balance of support and negotiation. If one thing goes wrong – like a childminder getting ill or a parent being unable to start the car – it can send this delicate set of arrangements crashing to the ground. Clearly, policy will never be able to clear up this messiness; nor should it aim to. Rather, the goal should be finding ways of working *with* that messiness, of accepting the unintended consequences and complex relationships between cause and effect that define everyday family life.

## 1. A new vision of public service and family support

Back in the early 1970s, when the Sex Discrimination Act was first introduced, government finally acknowledged that the reason for disparities at work did not rest with individual women and their so-called limitations, but rather with systemic and institutional barriers. The raft of legislation around discrimination and equality since then indicates that the state plays a crucial role in tackling some of those barriers that stood in the way of women, barriers that could never be overcome by individuals on their own.

Just as the state recognised its role in tackling sex discrimination in the workplace 30 years ago, so it must shape a role for itself in relation to family life today. That role is not one of prescription; nor is it one predicated on moralising about specific patterns of family life. Rather, just as the Sex Discrimination Act tried to do, it is about removing barriers, and offering positive support to families. It is about ensuring families can make decisions about how they can best combine employment and unpaid care in order to bring up their kids and maximise their life chances. This is the domestic politics of parenting.

But recognising that there is a legitimate and vital relationship between the state and family life does not add up to a call for a series of direct interventions based on rather crude means of public finance and compulsion alone. Intervention does not need to add up to intrusion. Instead we argue in this chapter that re-imagining public services, and focusing on how state and families can work together to *co-produce* the public good of future citizens, is a crucial part of the next wave of debates around the work–life balance.

Public services – what they are and what they are for – need to be redefined. Drives to 'join up' government, to tackle 'cross-cutting' matters such as social exclusion, regeneration and equality issues, all reflect the recognition that old silo-based models of policy-making and implementation do not work with the grain of people's needs. Much has been learned about how the state might intervene in complex social issues – including the complicated activities that constitute everyday family life – even in the period since Labour came to power in 1997.

Recent debates about public service reform have centred on the need to *personalise* services, to start with the people who are supposed to be benefiting from state provision and design services around their needs. Implicit within this agenda is the acknowledgement that mass-produced, monolithic public service institutions are unlikely to serve modern purposes or to alleviate some of the complex social challenges we now face. The explosion in social marketing and the consensus across government departments that the toughest challenge for administrations rests with changing people's behaviour are driving shifts in how the nature of 'public service' is understood.

As Andrew Turnbull, former cabinet secretary, said in 2003:

> *We can't succeed in improving your health unless we enlist you; we can't achieve better standards in schools if families aren't with us; we can't achieve safe neighbourhoods unless we can mobilise local communities.*[92]

So, public services need to be understood less in terms of deliverables and more in terms of *helping people to help themselves*. This reflects a long tradition in progressive politics; the prize to be claimed is less about creating a perfect set of public service institutions, and more about how services can help people to transform their lives and, ultimately, themselves. The goal is to find ways of supporting individuals, of providing scaffolding to their lives. The state should not be trying to do everything itself; making this its purpose would result in failure.

This shift in the public service model – from 'do unto' to 'working together' – remains patchy. Even in its thinking about parents specifically, this government continues to oscillate uneasily between empowering parents (for example, the education white paper's unerring focus on 'parent power') and punishing them for poor parenting (for example, arresting parents when their children truant).

The current state of play in public policy can be illustrated in the following way:

|  | Direct intervention | Indirect intervention |
| --- | --- | --- |
| Problem-centred model | Parenting orders[93] | Anti-poverty measures[94] |
| Person-centred model | Children's centres[95] | Right to flexible working[96] |

Our recommendations focus on how government can get its story straight about parents, and develop a new relationship with families that draws on models of public service based on co-production and user-led innovation.

Co-production is the only model of public services that will unlock the energy currently being invested with too little effect in debates about work–life balance and families. Families are complex adaptive systems whose form is made up and influenced by the interactions of a whole host of positive and negative dynamics. The goal of government should be to support the positive forces associated with the production of the shared goods of family life, and reduce or minimise the negative ones (eg low income, mental illness, poor quality relationships).

So what might this look like in practice? Government and other organisations need to find opportunities to invest in development and research that investigates in greater depth and clarity the opportunities for family service redesign. This is less about designing new institutional forms to meet the needs of families, and more about reconfiguring existing touch points, intermediary organisations and channels that families use, to ensure that they reflect more accurately the needs and interests of those families.

In the meantime we have three examples of how such a 'service redesign' approach to family policy might help government to focus on helping families to help themselves. As these examples illustrate, the approach we propose here is based on the government working to encourage a shift in public culture as much as making direct interventions itself.

**Family life vouchers**
What people count as 'family' varies massively, making it a problematic analytical category. Notions of 'family activity' are affected by the subjective use of 'family' as a category as well. It would be easy to assume that at its most basic, families bring up children, and activities such as feeding, bathing and giving love form core activities to be carried out within families. But it has always been the case that families outsource a range of activities to get them done. In 1711, the *Spectator* ran an article about the growing trend in women outsourcing that sacred cow of modern motherhood, breastfeeding. The article commented that 'the mother who pretends indisposition will soon persuade the good man to send the child to the nurse'.[97] It was common practice in the eighteenth century to send babies to wet nurses. Rather than being seen as unpaid reproductive labour, breastfeeding became a form of paid labour.

As highlighted in chapter 3, trends in outsourcing have continued. Currently, childcare vouchers enable parents to outsource the most significant of family activities. We recommend that the purpose of these vouchers should be expanded, and repositioned as 'family life vouchers'. Parents would be free to decide what elements of family activity they wanted to outsource based on their own values and the different emphases people place on the whole range of chores and childrearing responsibilities that make up everyday family life.

Some parents may choose to spend them on cleaning, to give them more 'quality time' with their children. Others may use the vouchers to cover the costs of transport from their child's school if they are unable to get there on time to pick them up. Others still may decide that the best thing for their family is to put the vouchers towards an after-school activity or Saturday club that enables their children to get involved in local sporting or cultural activities. As all these examples demonstrate, 'family life vouchers' would empower parents to make decisions that are genuinely in their children's interests, rather than basing those decisions on expediency, necessity or the impact of external factors.

This recommendation draws on recent developments in policy around support for disabled people. Direct payments – in principle at least – were introduced to give disabled people the funds and power to commission their own support. Making childcare vouchers 'family life vouchers' would reflect a similar shift in family policy, designed to empower families themselves in deciding what kind of support to build around their lives.

## Public value inspection framework for childcare

Clearly, many families will continue to choose to outsource elements of their childcare. Though welcome, the commitment to expand childcare provision will not provide families with the hoped-for choice if parents are not reassured about the quality of that provision.

This is particularly true in the context of increasingly shrill debates about the impact of formal childcare on child development. Debates have rumbled for many years now about the significance for children of their mothers' working, and, while the evidence is inconclusive, particularly once children have reached the age of 12 months, for many parents outsourcing childcare is a source of guilt and worry.

We believe that the debate about formal childcare needs to shift in its focus – from worrying about how it is organised, or how to expand provision, to emphasising instead the *qualities* of care that is provided. Bearing in mind the argument we have made here – about the primary purpose of families to work together to create public value – the critical factor in outsourced childcare is the extent to which it mirrors and supports the creation of these public goods. A new inspection and assessment framework should be developed for childcare providers – from private childminders to extended schools – based on the various elements of the public goods we identified in chapter 1. For example, to what extent does childcare nurture, respect and empower children? To what extent does it foster an eagerness to learn? To what extent does it help children to become autonomous and self-aware human beings? A public value framework for childcare, that goes well beyond basic health and safety concerns, may help to allay parental fears that outsourcing the most precious element of family life – childrearing – will have long-term consequences for their children.

**Employers re-imagine themselves as 'extended family'**
A universal service to help families help themselves is unlikely to be effective if there are not strong partnerships between families, advocacy organisations, state institutions and employers. Therefore how employers behave is important in re-imagining public services for families.

Earlier in this report we noted the trend towards employers casting themselves as 'home-from-homes' offering services that both helped employees sort out difficulties or chores, but also increased efficiency and productivity overall. There has been a proliferation of work-based gyms, concierges, subsidised bars and crèches.

We recommend that employers should shift their metaphor. Rather than positioning themselves as 'home-from-home' they should re-cast themselves as extended family. Seeing themselves as extended families will ensure that employers are better aligned with the views families hold both about the place of paid work and their preferences in childcare. This might mean they don't invest in a workplace nursery, but instead fund a network of childminders who look after children in the comfort and regularity of their own homes or book a number of places at nurseries where staff live and then offer financial assistance in meeting the costs of the places if they are taken up.

## 2. Open up a public conversation about parents

In 2003, a new reality TV format was born with the arrival on our screens of *Wifeswap*. As the website claims: 'The series lifts the lid on the choices different people make: how they divide up parenting, shopping and housework, spending priorities and what they want from their social life.'[98] The series, which attracted a record-breaking six million viewers to Channel 4, offered people a unique opportunity to look inside other families and understand how other people prioritised the activities and resources within their homes.

*Wifeswap* had a ready-made audience. How often do we get the chance to look inside other people's families at that level of everyday life? Our research supports the huge viewing figures for *Wifeswap* in suggesting that there is a massive unmet demand for families to discover more opportunities to learn from one another, looking at how others juggle the interaction of paid and unpaid care.

Families at the moment remain caught in what we might call the 'tyranny of relativism'. On the one hand they recognise the public story that is told about the end of the typically constituted family. On the other, they call their families 'typical' and 'average'. This apparent paradox uncovers a nervousness to challenge the norms of family habits, and a lack of opportunities to learn from other models of combining and integrating paid and unpaid work.

What *Wifeswap* offers is the *possibility* that things could be organised differently. Simply opening up this sense of possibility enables parents and families to make their own scripts more explicit, and to question why they are organising themselves in the way they do. Increasing negotiation and conversation about how paid and unpaid work are allocated helps to ensure that the ways in which families organise themselves are optimised for the co-production of shared goods.

It is crucial to get the medium as well as the message right. A public information campaign about family scripts is unlikely to catch on in the same way that *Wifeswap* had people glued to their TV screens. As an object that features heavily in most family days, the television (which Paul Ginsborg has called the 'new hearth')[99] represents a powerful and popular medium that connects families to national and international debates. Seeing *Wifeswap* as part of the public service broadcasting quota and imagining ways of complementing and supporting this format is a first step towards a broader public conversation designed to open up the scripts of family life.

### 3. Build negotiating capacity through peer support

Lots of the families we spoke to hinted that the negotiation of their roles had been a conversation that had never translated into action.

> We did think about me staying at home but we never really firmed it up.
>
> Father

> It causes an argument when he has to do what we're supposed to do as parents.
>
> Mother

> I kept on handing over control but it kept on coming back.
>
> Mother

Fear of relationship breakdown and a lack of sense of possibility about how things could be different are major factors in fixing family scripts. Finding ways of making these scripts explicit, and enabling families to interrogate them, question them, and talk about whether there could be a better way of producing the shared goods of family life, will be a critical part of helping families to help themselves.

But families are very sensitive about who they are willing to open up these scripts with. Parents have always believed that they have most to learn from other parents, rather than professionals.

> We don't need professionals to tell us how to be good parents.
>
> Mother

> *I take more notice of my mum than I do of the welfare. She's had eight and we're alright . . . you've got more confidence in your mother than you would have in the advice they'd give you.*[100]

Investing in peer networks of parents would support families who are trying to understand how best to bring up their kids. Rather than advocating for more direct interventions, we recommend that the state provides support – via schools, advocacy organisations such as Gingerbread and Netmums for networks of parents to help each other.

This model of state support recognises that there is no such thing as an 'ideal' parent; in these terms state interventions need to be less focused on 'teaching' parenting and more focused on providing information and creating learning opportunities.

> **Case study: Netmums (www.netmums.com)**
> Netmums is a family of websites run by volunteer mums living in the local area. These online forums were set up in 2000 to offer other parents (including dads) support, and to enable members to share advice about family life and the community they live in. There are currently 110,000 members in 80 different towns and cities in the UK, and members provide much of the content of their local website. Netmums was established partly to counter the isolation and uncertainty which many mums experienced in the absence of an extended family living nearby; according to their research 61 per cent of mums surveyed don't see their family enough or would like to see more of them. Similarly, 67 per cent of mums said they were more likely to turn to a friend, website or a book for advice than to a family member.
> 
> From recommending family-friendly restaurants to practical tips on meeting other parents, these websites provide the sort of word-of-mouth information that mums lacking extensive support networks have difficulty accessing. Popular features of the site include the 'Meet a mum' message board for parents living in the

> same community. Help is also on offer for mums with health worries, those wanting to return to work and others in search of local information about organisations like Mind or NCT. This is an online forum designed by parents for parents in order meet their needs.
> Along with signing petitions members respond to wide-ranging surveys on subjects such as work, wellbeing and postnatal depression. As a result, Netmums has become an influential campaigning organisation delivering the views of parents to policy-makers.

It is clear that some families learn the art of negotiation over time:

> *When we had our second kid, he started to do more, he's done his part and I think things will stay like this now we've got two.*
> Mother

> *If I'm going to have another child, I said you'll need to make an effort to be around more.... Before I left everything up to him, there was only one boss, one head of family, and now there's two.*
> Mother

> *That's what helps the family to work, when you have understanding, you both jump around to make things work.*
> Father

> *At times it felt like we talked of nothing else.*
> Father

This is about finding ways of building family capacity to constantly challenge themselves about the organisation of paid and unpaid labour. Investing in the peer–parent networks that create the space to make these challenges is a crucial step in re-energising the work–life balance debate.

## 4. Invest in quality relationships

It is the *quality* of relationships rather than the formal categories they belong to that matters most for families.[101] The costs of poor relationships are felt in every part of the welfare state infrastructure – from benefits, insurance, criminal justice, drug and alcohol abuse.[102] Supporting people's capacity to build good long-term relationships will help to ensure that family units can continue to create the public value we hope for.

Building good relationships is not about moral exhortation or coercion, rather it is about recognising that people enter partnerships with hope and aspirations for a positive future together. The assumption that people know how to look after their relationships and their families is misleading: most people learn through making mistakes.

Yet many people still consider that asking for advice on a relationship before it has broken down anticipates failure, rather than maintains success. Fears of paternalism and didacticism have led to relationship support becoming a sensitive subject. The result is that a crucial component of family life has been neglected.

As this report has documented, modern relationships face a challenging range of pressures. Caught between longer hours at work and ever more demanding parenting standards it is often relationships that become the casualties of the 'time squeeze'. For a growing number of couples these difficulties are compounded by the particular problems reconstituted families face in housing a range of different norms under one roof. Step-families are most likely to break down in the first year when these difficulties are at their most intense.

To tackle the stigma around asking for relationship support, the dominant cultural model of marriage – that it is based on romantic love – needs to be countered. The reality is that good quality relationships need work, patience and self-awareness. Fostering long-term relationships – particularly when they involve children – is a complex and skilled job that requires people to learn new skills and approaches to living with others.

There is some evidence that families themselves are open to acknowledging this. In the absence of extended family bonds and community networks couples are more willing to look outside the traditional sources of advice to mediation services. In our focus groups we found that the idea of more support was appealing particularly to women.

*People need help with their relationships, sometimes it's easier to speak to a stranger than a friend.*
Mother

However, people can struggle to make contact with these organisations before already making the decision to separate; all too often mediation at the point of divorce can represent the first opportunity to openly discuss and negotiate differences.

People need to be offered as many opportunities as possible to invest in their relationships. To that end we recommend the following.

### Increase government subsidies for organisations working on relationships and family support

While there have been some positive developments, relationship support funding has been moved around government so much and re-categorised so frequently that it has not had the attention it deserves.[103] Couples need to able to focus solely on their relationship rather than being spoken to only as parents – family support does not always equate to relationship support.

### Make private relationship counselling tax deductible

A more consistent approach to public funding is vital, and making private relationship counselling tax deductible would be another significant move in the right direction. The government needs to recognise the long-term social benefits of helping relationships in the early stages; it could be seen as comparable to the committed investment in preventative family planning of the 1960s.

### Introduce supported self-assessment for parents

Rather than telling couples how to conduct their relationships and deciding on the support that they need, government needs to recognise that couples themselves are best placed to determine the help they need, when they need it and how they want it to be delivered.

Self-assessment should be introduced so that people are able to gain access to the right services at the right time. For example, in the first year following a baby's birth health support is well established, but the focus is rarely on the adult relationship, despite the fact it is often under intense pressure.[104] There are good models of support during this period that can be learned from. An example is the PIPPIN programme, which is designed to prepare couples for the emotional strain before they have a child, equipping them with coping strategies.

Furthermore, relationship support could be embedded in existing 'touch points' and frontline services such as GP surgeries, health visitors, midwives and education so that couples are not required to search out the help they need.

## 5. Involve dads

Chapter 3 documented the 'quiet revolution' in fathers' attitudes and aspirations in relation to family life. As we argued there, systemic and institutional barriers risk keeping this revolution behind the front door and locked inside male aspirations within individual families, rather than being translated into action. There remain too few opportunities for men to express their desires beyond the household. We need to engineer a tipping point that involves the state, media and other civic institutions catching up with what people value, and finding ways of helping people to enact those values.

In part, this involves the government toughening up its attitude to male responsibility for care. Its approach so far has rested either on carrots or a financial stick. Government needs to recognise its part in creating the system that families are currently constrained by. The state is not a passive actor: while policy remains predominantly based on a model where women are the primary carers it is too easy to assume that work–life balance debates and responsibility for childrearing are 'women's issues'. Of course, as our research indicates, this is still the case for many families. But part of the state catching up with the quiet revolution involves it challenging notions of motherhood and fatherhood.

However, engineering a tipping point is not straightforward; it does not translate into a simple and single policy intervention. Instead, the focus needs to be on how existing institutional patterns and practices could be changed and developed in order to create a sense of momentum and possibility. As Doug McAdam has argued, 'It is there in the existing associational groups of networks of the aggrieved community that the first groping steps are taken towards collective action.'[105] So what might this approach look like in practice?

### Make mums the agitators of the revolution

Research indicates that mothers, more than anyone or anything else, may be the key intermediaries and agitators in bringing about this revolution. A study undertaken by the National Centre on Fathers and Families in the United States concluded that there was a trend for fathers and father figures to spend more time in Head Start, a pre-kindergarten programme, if the mother was highly involved.[106] Similarly recent research in the UK with the DfES Fathers Advisory Group found that maternal involvement in learning was a more significant factor in father involvement than either the educational qualifications of each parent or the quality of the parental relationship.[107]

### Design collective activities based on existing patterns

Involving dads will never become a reality while the debate remains at a theoretical level. The relationship between attitudes and behaviour is not one way: changing behaviour can shift attitudes as well. Research by Working Families suggests that fathers are far more likely to become involved in family life after engaging in collective activities with other fathers.[108] Finding ways of supporting father-focused activities will be a crucial part of creating a tipping point.

Designing these activities based on existing patterns will also help. Through our research one area where men genuinely seem to be equally involved in relation to their children is health. Fathers we met shared their concerns about their kids getting the right food, doing exercise and being healthy generally. Parents whose children suffered from long-term health conditions shared the additional care load associated with these illnesses. Finding ways of building on these patterns around the medicine cabinet and sports field will help to ensure that the involvement of fathers starts with where they are at, rather than from where policy is at.

**Start early and keep dads involved**
Rather than a 'big bang' approach, the key to unlocking this quiet revolution is a focus on the small but regular patterns that can be designed into family life and support services to engage dads. Women we spoke to felt that the biggest gain from paternity leave was the opportunity it offered to help fathers understand how much work goes in to a 'day at home'. Combined with pre- and postnatal support services that focus more on building fathers' confidence, it presents an opportunity for fathers to learn to make connections across the different elements of family life, so that parents can learn to share the mental burden of running a family.

Ongoing engagement will be crucial. Already a handful of innovative schools are experimenting with 'dads and lads' sessions – often introduced in an attempt to improve boys' performance in school, but with the additional result that schools are beginning to create spaces for fathers to parent together and talk about their experiences as dads in a 'safe place'. We recommend that, just as many workplaces run a 'take your daughter to work' day, all schools should run a 'take your dad to school' day as a first step in the right direction.

## 6. Experiment at work

Earlier in this report we argued that current approaches to flexible working are too static. Taking a life-cycle or person-centric view of flexibility highlights the need to focus not only on finding new ways of getting work done, but also on enabling parents to move between different working patterns depending on the demands of their families. Children's needs change over time and employers should learn new ways, not only to offer flexible patterns, but also to be able to move between different patterns at different stages of people's careers and family life.

Many employers are yet to be convinced of the 'business case' for offering more flexible working patterns, despite the increasingly unarguable evidence that enabling people to blend work and life is one of the most effective routes to releasing people's potential. The valuable work of campaigning organisations such as Working Families in beginning to make this business case cannot be underestimated.

However, we believe that more needs to be done. The two recommendations put forward here would help to shift and deepen the debate about flexible working, grounding it in the realities of everyday family life.

### Broaden the repertoire of flexible working

Current flexible working patterns are overwhelmingly confined to part-time work, with options such as job sharing taking up a mere 2 per cent of the working population who are not full-time staff.[109] Yet many people – whether they are employers or employees – note the difficulties of getting some jobs done part time. There is an urgent need to broaden our repertoire of flexibility as part of an approach to supporting families on their own terms.

The need to experiment with new forms of flexible working is made nearly impossible, however, by the current climate of ignorance and fear that surrounds shifts in working patterns on the part of both employers and employees.[110] Highly publicised tribunals and court cases have created a culture of low risk taking and poor dialogue about what works between staff and organisations. This is compounded by a piecemeal and complex set of laws that govern this area of working life. Workers can request the right to work flexibly; the employer must consider this request but can still turn it down.

Solutions would be far more likely to emerge if they could be co-constructed between the member of staff and the employer. The current legal framework has created a culture of antagonism between employers and employees, where honest conversation about what's needed for the business, and how these needs could be met in more creative ways, are little more than a distant dream.

The consequences of such rigidity and confrontation rather than collaboration should not be underestimated. Growing numbers of people are reaching the conclusion that they simply cannot achieve the kind of balance they seek between paid and unpaid work within organisations; in other words, more people are making personal choices about work, identity and what it means to achieve success, and concluding that 'exit' is their best option.

### Learn from the people who have 'opted out'

The growing number of people choosing to take less pressurised roles has thrown into question older formations about how professional success is defined, and casts new light on the tired debate around 'work–life balance'. People are seeking to create 'third-way' integrated lifestyles as home-based micro-entrepreneurs, freelancers and consultants. For many people, this rejection of the old models of work–life balance is cause for celebration. Sahar Hashemi, one of the co-founders of Coffee Republic, described in an interview why she quit her City job to start up her own business:

> I wanted work that lets me be myself. . . . There used to be two options: a career or kids. Either or. In the gap in between is where the women entrepreneurs are. They're reinventing work for women.[111]

And, as our own research hinted at, it is women leading the way in this trend. Research carried out by Cranfield School of Management supports the view that women hold different values and aspirations from their male counterparts, and are driven by the pursuit of personal fulfilment and making a difference, rather than job titles, pay rises or promotions.[112] Women, Dame Judith Mayhew has suggested, 'drop out because they can. We've always had more choices, and we have many definitions of "success", not just one. In many ways it's men who are trapped.'[113]

Given the 'quiet revolution' that we have already documented, it is a matter of urgency that lessons are learned from this generation of 'missing women'. Employers need to be encouraged and supported in thinking about how they can begin to mainstream some of the working practices that women felt they needed to leave organisations in order to achieve.

# 7. Endnote

## Where next for work–life balance debates?

*People want simplistic explanations and solutions to complex problems, resulting in pragmatic solutions concentrated on government legislation and workplace policies.*[114]

The relationship between paid and unpaid work in family life represents a new frontier of the welfare state. Men and women alike are reporting a desire to spend more time with their families, while simultaneously needing and wanting to work for both the income and the satisfaction jobs can provide. The modern family faces a daily pattern of negotiating and juggling the full range of activities that add up to being a family.

Recently the government has started to talk about supporting 'hard-working families', in recognition of the fact that levels of frustration about perceived barriers or lack of support for families has become a major voting issue. Despite almost daily proclamations that families are in terminal decline, all the indicators suggest that people are still investing tremendous energy and hope in creating family life, in some cases over and over again. As a society, we need this energy. As demonstrated in chapter 1, the impact of the family setting on who we become is significant. Helping families to produce public goods is crucial.

Yet the energy families give to childrearing represents an unrecognised, undervalued resource.

# Endnote

*Care work may be loving, but the work itself has no public recognition; it is an invisible gift, and many of the men and women who do it feel they have dropped out of the adult society of their peers.*[115]

Paid work is at the heart of how we measure productivity and the health of the economy. Unpaid care work – vital as it is – remains unrecognised. Family life is best described as a gift economy: people in families willingly give up their time and energy to love and nurture one another.

One response to supporting family life is to turn family activity from a gift economy to a market economy through providing the kinds of activities and nurture that families have traditionally given each other through the market; through turning what might be called reproductive labour into productive labour through expanding the childcare market and providing more incentives for parents to get back into paid, full-time work.

For many, this alone is not an appealing option. It eats away at the heart of family life and assumes that it is possible to put a price on everything. But what it does highlight – and this has been at the core of this pamphlet – is that there is no such thing as free care, only paid and unpaid care.

This pamphlet is not a moral argument about what families should do. It is a political argument about an approach that enables all families to flourish on their own terms. Finding ways of recognising the importance of family life, whatever form it takes, and designing supportive systems around those families, remains one of the biggest challenges for twenty-first-century progressive governments.

It is a challenge that is unlikely to be overcome unless the debate begins by comprehending what things looks like at the level of the family. Every family will organise itself differently: each of the families in our typology represent alternative adaptive responses to the challenge of organising paid and unpaid work. Gaining a deeper understanding of the cast of British families will be essential in strengthening the connections between those families, state and civil society. That has been the focus of this report. The question remains: where is this agenda going?

We believe that there is much that can be learned from families themselves. In beginning to solve the immediate challenges of work and family life, people are starting to generate some new answers to much deeper questions about what kind of lives we want to lead. The mothers and fathers we spoke to were clear that care for them was an *investment*, rather than a negative balance on the productivity sheet. They were clear about the connections between home and work, about the trade-offs and compromises that needed to be made in the interests of creating a positive family setting.

Frustration, when it was expressed, was not about not being able to 'have it all'. Instead it was about the need for employers and the state to share the burden of caring responsibilities with families. Too often, people felt they were carrying the weight of their family on their own shoulders while knowing how important good parenting is not only to their children but also to the rest of us.

There is very little language or vocabulary to explore this dimension of life. But society needs to adjust its acoustics fast, and begin to listen to what families themselves are saying about family life. This will become only more urgent in coming years. The demographic changes of an ageing population, longer life expectancy and declining birth rate mean that more and more people will find themselves caring for elderly relatives and parents. We will be relying more than ever on unpaid care as a population. Unless the value of both paid and unpaid work can be knitted together more effectively, those with caring responsibilities will continue to lack the necessary support and recognition that such vital and demanding work deserves.

As Richard Reeves has argued, we are in danger of creating economy-friendly families, rather than a family-friendly economy.[116] Understanding each family's hopes, aspirations and need for support might help to right this balance and discover a new narrative about the relationship between paid and unpaid care. Seven in ten people believe that men's and women's lives are becoming more similar in terms of the need to balance family and employment.

This represents a potentially new alliance for change, grown out of the stresses and strains men and women report in keeping their families going every day. Coupling these feelings with broader debates about wellbeing, control and autonomy in the face of seemingly insuperable forces of commercialisation, capitalism and consumerism may offer a means of rebalancing the significance we accord to paid and unpaid work. Starting with families themselves will give us a new language – not one about moral exhortation or political correctness – about the public value of family life to everyone.

# Appendix A
## List of project interviews, held 2005–6

| | |
|---|---|
| 17 November | Duncan Fisher, Fathers Direct |
| 24 November | Mary Crowley, Parenting Education and Support Forum |
| 25 November | Purniam Tanuku, National Day Nurseries Association |
| 28 November | Sally Russell, Netmums |
| 01 December | Clem Henricson, National Families and Parenting Institute |
| 05 December | Ros Edwards, London South Bank University |
| 08 December | Gwen Vaughn, Gingerbread |
| 13 December | Chris Pond and Alison Garnham, National Council for One Parent Families |
| 10 January | Val Gillies, London South Bank University |
| 11 January | Kathleen Healy, Freshfields |
| 31 January | Deborah Shead, Mediation UK |
| 22 February | Martin Williams, Department for Education and Skills |
| 27 February | Naomi Eisenstadt, Department for Education and Skills |
| 02 March | Susan Hay, Bright Horizons / Working Families |
| 28 March | Ray Shostak, HM Treasury |

# Appendix B
## List of attendees at the project seminar – 13 March 2006

| | |
|---|---|
| Susan Hay | Bright Horizons Family Solutions |
| Naomi Eisenstadt | Department for Education and Skills |
| David Darton | Equal Opportunities Commission |
| Jenny Watson | Equal Opportunities Commission |
| David Pearce | HM Treasury |
| Efe Abebe | Munro and Forster |
| Dave Roberts | Munro and Forster |
| Catherine Wrigley | Munro and Forster |
| Alison Garnham | National Council for One Parent Families |
| Clem Henricson | National Family and Parenting Institute |
| Sally Russell | Netmums |
| Mary Crowley | Parenting and Education Support Forum |
| Tim Kahn | Pre-School Learning Alliance |
| Ed Straw | PricewaterhouseCoopers LL |
| Richard Stubbins | Sanofi Pasteur MSD |
| Julie Tiley | Sanofi Pasteur MSD |
| Veronique Walsh | Sanofi Pasteur MSD |
| Ros Edwards | South Bank University |
| Val Gillies | South Bank University |
| Rebecca Gill | Trade Union Congress |
| Jonathan Swan | Working Families |
| Rebecca Fauth | Work Foundation |

# Appendix C
## The research process

Between November 2005 and March 2006 we undertook a series of interviews with experts across the fields of academia, policy campaigning and practice; see Appendix A for a full list. These conversations helped us to clarify the questions that we put to 620 parents to help us to pinpoint our areas of focus and start to clarify the framework for our in-depth research with parents. The GfK NOP Random Location Omnibus conducted the survey at 175 sampling points across the country with quotas for age and sex within working status, social class, marital status, parental status and age of child.

In the second phase of the research we interviewed a range of 12 families from across the socioeconomic spectrum, of different ages and stages in family life, from different ethnic backgrounds and in various states of employment. If there were two partners in the household we spoke to them separately using a combination of questions and activities to build up a picture of family life. These conversations and the diaries that the families filled in, detailing the activities that made up their day-to-day life, form the backbone of our findings. We are very grateful to those families who invited us into their homes and took their time to take part in our research.

We built on the findings from these in-depth interviews with a series of focus groups, speaking to another 30 mums and dads with dependent children. We used these focus groups to test our findings and develop our analysis. The stories and quotes that we have

## Appendix C

included have all been drawn from this research and have been anonymised.

Finally, we held a seminar to share our findings and analysis with the experts whom we had consulted at the beginning of the project and other key individuals to help us clarify and sharpen our argument and recommendations.

# Notes

1. Equal Opportunities Commission research findings have shown 86% of fathers and 31% of mothers to be working full-time. Equal Opportunities Commission, *Fathers: Balancing work and family* (Manchester: EOC, 2003).
2. Quoted in R Reeves, *Dad's Army: The case for father-friendly workplaces* (London: The Work Foundation, 2002); available at www.theworkfoundation.com/pdf/5110000046.pdf (accessed 2 Apr 2006).
3. K Fisher, A McCulloch and J Gershuny, *British Fathers and Children: A report for Channel 4 'Dispatches'* (Colchester: University of Essex, Institute of Social and Economic Research, 1999); quoted in M Bunting, *Willing Slaves: Why the overwork culture is killing us* (New York: Harper Collins, 2004).
4. See www.publicservantlifestyle.co.uk/dynamic/sections/family_friends/article_display.php?id=183 (accessed 5 Apr 2006).
5. Quoted in Bunting, *Willing Slaves*.
6. Office for National Statistics, 'How UK fills its day: mostly sleeping, eating, watching TV', 2000 Time Use Survey (London: ONS, 2002); available at www.statistics.gov.uk/cci/nugget.asp?id=7 (accessed 2 Apr 2006). It shows that sleeping, eating and watching TV take up more than half the day.
7. Office for National Statistics online, 'Adults living with their parents: by sex and age', *Social Trends* 34, available at www.statistics.gov.uk/STATBASE/ssdataset.asp?vlnk=7261 (accessed 2 Apr 2006). In spring 2003 nearly three-fifths of men aged 20–24 lived with their parents, compared with half in 1991. For women the proportion of 20–24-year-olds living with their parents increased from a third to nearly two-fifths.
8. Netmums, 'A mum's life' survey available at www.netmums.com/cpg/mumslife/mumslife.htm (accessed 2 Apr 2006). It found that 75% of mums cite 'lack of time for me' as the most stressful part of their day-to-day life.
9. Quoted in A Wolf, 'Working girls', *Prospect*, Apr 2006.
10. C Deforges and A Abouchaar, *The Impact of Parental Involvement, Parental Support and Family Education on Pupil Achievement and Adjustment: A*

*literature review*, Department for Education and Skills Research Report 433 (Norwich: The Stationery Office, 2003).
11. D Goleman, *Emotional Intelligence: Why it can matter more than IQ* (New York: Bantam Books, 1995).
12. W Hutton, 'Employers and work–life balance', see website for the Work Foundation on the future of work–life balance at www.employersforworklifebalance.org.uk/will_hutton.htm (accessed 3 Apr 2006).
13. H Meltzer et al, *The Mental Health of Children and Adolescents in Great Britain* (London: The Stationery Office, 2000).
14. S Mahtani and MH Bond, 'A critical look at parenting research from the mainstream: problems uncovered while adapting research to non-western cultures', *British Journal of Developmental Psychology* 20 (2002).
15. S Zuboff and J Maxmin, *The Support Economy: Why corporations are failing individuals and the next episode of capitalism* (London: Penguin Press, 2003).
16. H Bosanquet, 'Wages and housekeeping' in CS Loch (ed), *Methods of Social Advance* (1904).
17. A Johnson, speech given in response to the Work and Families Bill, 10 Oct 2005.
18. Social Exclusion Unit, A Better Education for Children in Care – Practice Guides (London: Office of the Deputy Prime Minister, nd), available at www.socialexclusionunit.gov.uk/publications.asp?did=189 (accessed 3 Apr 2006).
19. *The Equalities Review: Interim report for consultation* (London: Cabinet Office, 2006), available at www.theequalitiesreview.org.uk/publications/index.asp (accessed 3 Apr 2006).
20. Ibid.
21. Ibid.
22. P McCarthy, K Laing and J Walker, *Offenders of the Future? Assessing the risk of children and young people becoming involved in criminal or antisocial behaviour* (London: DfES, 2004).
23. Quoted in P Diamond, S Katwala and M Munn (eds), *Family Fortunes: The new politics of childhood* (London: Fabian Society, 2004).
24. M Moore, *Creating Public Value: Strategic management in government* (Cambridge, MA: Harvard University Press, 1995).
25. B Bozeman, 'Public value failure: when efficient markets may not work', *Public Administration Review* 62, no 2 (Mar/Apr 2002).
26. M Midgley, *Utopias, Dolphins and Computers: Problems of philosophical plumbing* (London: Routledge, 1996).
27. P Hennessy, *The Hidden Wiring: Power, politics and the constitution* (London: Fabian Society, 1990).
28. A personal view from a father quoted on www.forparentsbyparents.com (accessed 3 Apr 2006).
29. EOC, *Fathers*.
30. For more details see www.adviceguide.org.uk/n6w/index/life/employment/parental_rights_at_work.htm (accessed 3 Apr 2006).

31  See for example Wolf, 'Working girls'.
32  Hutton, 'Employers and work–life balance'.
33  A Jones, *About Time for Change* (London: Work Foundation, 2003).
34  See www.eoc.org.uk (accessed 3 Apr 2006).
35  See www.daycaretrust.org.uk/index.php (accessed 5 Apr 2006).
36  Ibid.
37  For more details see www.statistics.gov.uk/downloads/theme_labour/Keyindicatorsofwomen_LMT Oct.pdf (accessed 5 Apr 2006).
38  C Fagan, A Hegewisch and J Pillinger, *Out of Time: Why Britain needs a new approach to working-time flexibility* (London: Trades Union Congress: 2006), available at www.tuc.org.uk/extras/outoftime.pdf (accessed 3 Apr 2006).
39  Polling completed for this research by GfK NOP Random Location Omnibus; see Appendix C for more details.
40  M Evans and J Eyre, *The Opportunities of a Lifetime: Model lifetime analysis of current British social policy* (Bristol: Policy Press for the Joseph Rowntree Foundation, 2004).
41  Department of Trade and Industry, *Work and Parents: Competitiveness and choice*, green paper, Cm 5005 (Norwich: HMSO, 2000), available at www.dti.gov.uk/er/g_paper/pdfs/wpgreen.pdf (accessed 5 Apr 2006).
42  I La Valle et al, *Happy Families? Atypical work and its influence on family life* (Bristol: Policy Press for Joseph Rowntree Foundation, 2002).
43  M Barnes and C Bryson, *Keep Time for Children: The incidence of weekend working* (London: National Centre for Social Research, funded by The Relationships Foundation, 2004).
44  R Taylor, *The Future of Work–Life Balance* (Swindon: Economic and Social Research Council, 2002), quoted in Bunting, *Willing Slaves*.
45  See www.netmums.com/lc/postnataldepression_survey.php (accessed 4 Apr 2006).
46  See www.eoc.org.uk/PDF/time_use_and_childcare.pdf (accessed 3 Apr 2006).
47  D Buckingham, *After the Death of Childhood: Growing up in the age of electronic media* (London: Polity Press, 2000).
48  M Riddell, 'Ms Hewitt, you blew it', *Observer*, 25 Nov 2001, available at http://observer.guardian.co.uk/comment/story/0,6903,605567,00.html (accessed 3 Apr 2006).
49  Jones, *About Time for Change*.
50  See www.cartoonbank.com/product_details.asp?mscssid=V9MNSDKV9UPM9KMD55SEQ11JV6WM09K6&sitetype=1&did=4&sid=70634&whichpage=4&sortBy=popular&keyword=nanny&section=cartoons (accessed 5 Apr 2006).
51  See for example www.natcen.ac.uk/natcen/pages/or_familiesandchildren.htm (accessed 3 Apr 2006).
52  'Just a nanny? She's likely to earn up to £28,000 – more than a newly qualified teachers or nurse', *Times*, 19 Jan 2006.
53  See www.ear.co.uk/ (accessed 3 Apr 2006).

## Notes

54 See www.publicservantlifestyle.co.uk/dynamic/sections/family_friends/article_display.php?id=183 (accessed 5 Apr 2006).
55 AR Hochschild, 'Rent a Mom and other services: markets, meanings and emotions', *International Journal of Work, Organisation and Emotion* 1, no 1 (2005).
56 A Hirschmann, *Exit, Voice and Loyalty: Responses to decline in firms, organizations and states* (New Haven, CT: Harvard University Press, 1972).
57 Thomas Coram Research Unit, Institute of Education, 'Study highlights "unsustainable" fall in the number of childminders', press release, May 2001, available at www.jrf.org.uk/pressroom/releases/020500.asp (accessed 5 Apr 2006), relates to A Mooney et al, *Who cares? Childminding in the 1990s* (York: Joseph Rowntree Foundation, 2001).
58 See www.eoc.org.uk (accessed 3 Apr 2006).
59 A Bell and I La Valle, *Combining Self-employment and Family Life* (Bristol: Policy Press for the Joseph Rowntree Foundation, 2003).
60 See www.womenandequalityunit.gov.uk/women_work/key_facts.htm (accessed 3 Apr 2006).
61 EF Schumacher, *Small is Beautiful: Economics as if people mattered* (New York: Harper and Row, 1973).
62 See www.eoc.org.uk/PDF/time_use_and_childcare.pdf (accessed 3 Apr 2006).
63 Jones, *About Time for Change*.
64 'The Great British Time Survey', conducted by ICM and commissioned by CSV Make a Difference Day and Barclays (published Aug 2005), available at www.csv.org.uk/news/time+survey.htm (accessed 3 Apr 2006).
65 NOP Family and Equal Opportunities Commission, Young people and sex stereotyping data, Jan 2001. From 569 interviews with 11–16-year-olds in Great Britain completed through Young Generations Omnibus. Nationally representative with quotas set for age, sex, class and region.
66 nVision/FutureFoundation analysis done for the project on the British Household Panel Survey. Base 1000 adults, UK, 2004.
67 Fagan et al, *Out of Time*.
68 See www.womenandequalityunit.gov.uk (accessed 3 Apr 2006).
69 V Singh and S Vinnicombe, *The Female FTSE Index 2005* (Cranfield: Cranfield School of Management, 2005), see www.cranfield.ac.uk/som/research/centres/cdwbl/news.asp (accessed 3 Apr 2006).
70 'Mothers' job prospects are worst of all', *Observer*, 19 Mar 2006.
71 Office for National Statistics, *Labour Force Survey*, spring 2004 dataset (London: ONS, 2004).
72 Reeves, *Dad's Army*.
73 M O'Brien, *Shared Caring: Bringing fathers into the frame*, Working Paper 18 (London: Equal Opportunities Commission, 2005).
74 Fagan et al, *Out of Time*.
75 C Lasch, *Haven in a Heartless World* (New York: Basic Books, 1977).
76 See http://en.wikiquote.org/wiki/Margaret_Mead

77  A Buonfino and G Mulgan, 'Goodbye to all that', *Guardian*, 18 Jan 2006, see http://society.guardian.co.uk/communities/story/0,,1688280,00.html (accessed 3 Apr 2006).
78  B Jupp, *Living Together: Community life on mixed tenure estates* (London: Demos, 1999).
79  Quoted in B Brown and G Dench, 'Extended families: the heart of the private realm' in A Buofino and G Mulgan (eds), *Porcupines in Winter: The pleasures and pains of living together in modern Britain* (London: Young Foundation, 2006).
80  G Thomas and G Hocking, *Other People's Children: Why their quality of life is our concern* (London: Demos, 2003).
81  Interview with Mary Crowley, Jan 2006.
82  *Guardian*/ICM poll, Aug 2000.
83  See www.netmums.com/lc/restaurants.php (accessed 4 Apr 2006).
84  Future Foundation, *Paradoxical Parents*, report for the Children's Mutual (London: Future Foundation, 2003).
85  Quoted in Thomas and Hocking, *Other People's Children*.
86  R Green, 'Mentally ill parents and children's welfare', Information Briefing (London: National Society for the Prevention of Cruelty to Children, 2002).
87  'Isolation and loneliness: features of modern parenting', 8 Mar 2005; available at www.parentlineplus.org.uk/index.php?id=28&backPID=14&tt_news=36 (accessed 3 Apr 2006).
88  See www.youngminds.org.uk/parents/ (accessed 5 Apr 2006).
89  R Layard, *Mental Health: Britain's biggest social problem?* (London: Strategy Unit, Dec 2004).
90  Survey conducted by Netmums; available at www.netmums.com/lc/pndhistory_survey.php (accessed 4 Apr 2006).
91  See, for example, H Lownsbrough and D O'Leary, *The Leadership Imperative: Reforming children's services from the ground up* (London: Demos, 2005).
92  'The cabinet chief more West Wing than Yes, Minister', *Telegraph*, 12 Dec 2003.
93  A total of 5631 orders were made between March 2000 and December 2004. Quoted in G McNamara, 'Tackling anti-social behaviour: have we got it right?', an NCH briefing paper, 2005; available at www.nch.org.uk/uploads/documents/Tackling_anti_social_behaviour.pdf (accessed 4 Apr 2006).
94  The Childcare Tax Credit is being introduced in October. The Treasury estimates that it will benefit 1.5 million families. It will meet 70% of childcare costs to a maximum of £100 for one child and £150 for two or more children under the age of 14. New Deal for Lone Parents and Sure Start maternity grants reflect other enabling measures introduced in recent years.
95  There is a commitment to create 3500 children's centres by 2010. A National Family and Parenting Institute has been set up to coordinate local support for parents, and a National Parenting Academy has been set up to train professionals on how to work with parents.
96  The Work and Families Bill is expected to become law in April 2007. We have discussed its provisions in chapter 3.

## Notes

97  R Steele and J Addison, *Selections from the* Tatler *and the* Spectator, ed A Ross (London: Penguin Classics, 1997).
99  See www.channel4.com/life/microsites/W/wife_swap/ (accessed 4 Apr 2006).
99  P Ginsborg, *The Politics of Everyday Life: making choices, changing lives* (New Haven, CT: Yale University Press, 2005).
100 M Young and P Wilmott, *Family and Kinship in East London* (London: Routledge and Kegan Paul, 1957).
101 For example, Mansfield has argued that 'there is now compelling evidence to suggest that how parents get on – or don't get on – has a profound influence on children's lives', P Mansfield, 'The missing link in parenting education and support', *The Bulletin* 8, no 2 (May 2004). One meta-analysis of 68 family studies consistently found that good parenting is less likely to occur when the parents' relationship is troubled, O Erel and B Burnman, 'Interrelatedness of marital relations and parent–child relations: a meta-analytic review', *Psychological Bulletin* 118, no 1 (1995). Both are quoted in 'Relationship skills: the missing link in parenting education and support', available at www.scottishmarriagecare.org/Research/Briefing%202%20missing%20link.pdf (accessed 4 Apr 2006).
102 In Demos pamphlet *Relative Values*, Ed Straw estimated that the cost of 'broken homes' to society was £4 billion in 1998. E Straw, *Relative Values: Support for relationships and parenting* (London: Demos, 1998).
103 In 2002 the government produced 'Moving Forward Together', which identified existing problems with provision ('too little, too late') and proposed a government strategy for supporting relationships. Funding for relationship support, formerly known as MARS, stood at £3.2m in 2000 and had risen to £4.9m by 2005. In 2006 five existing grant schemes were combined into the Children, Young People and Families Grant Programme under which £17m will be allocated in 2006/07.
104 See for example 'The Relate Manifesto for strong couple and family relationships' available at www.relate.org.uk/Documents/Relate%20Manifesto.pdf (accessed 4 Apr 2006). Anecdotally, they believe that over 75% of their clients first found their relationship in difficulty after the birth of their first child.
105 M Diani and D McAdam (eds), *Social Movements and Networks: Relational approaches to collective action* (Oxford: Oxford University Press, 2003).
106 National Centre on Fathers and Families, see www.ncoff.gse.upenn.edu/ (accessed 5 Apr 2006).
107 R Goldman, *Fathers' Involvement in their Children's Education* (London: National Family and Parenting Institute, 2005).
108 Comment from Jonathan Swan, Working Families, at project seminar, see Appendix B.
109 See www.eoc.org.uk (accessed 4 Apr 2006).
110 For example, when Working Families took over Maternity Alliance's helpline, calls to the number tripled. This illustrates the lack of clarity and degree of concern people have about rights they are entitled to.

111 M Rice, 'The way women work', *Observer Magazine*, 14 Dec 2003.
112 Interview with S Vinnicombe, Cranfield School of Management, 2004, undertaken as part of the research for H McCarthy, *Girlfriends in High Places: How women's networks are changing the workplace* (London: Demos, 2004).
113 See http://news.bbc.co.uk/1/low/business/2296877.stm (accessed 5 Apr 2006).
114 S Lewis, R Rapoport and R Gambles, 'Reflections on the integration of paid work and the rest of life', *Journal of Managerial Psychology* 18, no 8 (2003).
115 R Sennett, *New Cultures of Capitalism* (New Haven, CT: Yale University Press, 2006).
116 Reeves, *Dad's Army*.

Copyright

## DEMOS – Licence to Publish

THE WORK (AS DEFINED BELOW) IS PROVIDED UNDER THE TERMS OF THIS LICENCE ("LICENCE"). THE WORK IS PROTECTED BY COPYRIGHT AND/OR OTHER APPLICABLE LAW. ANY USE OF THE WORK OTHER THAN AS AUTHORIZED UNDER THIS LICENCE IS PROHIBITED. BY EXERCISING ANY RIGHTS TO THE WORK PROVIDED HERE, YOU ACCEPT AND AGREE TO BE BOUND BY THE TERMS OF THIS LICENCE. DEMOS GRANTS YOU THE RIGHTS CONTAINED HERE IN CONSIDERATION OF YOUR ACCEPTANCE OF SUCH TERMS AND CONDITIONS.

1. **Definitions**
   a **"Collective Work"** means a work, such as a periodical issue, anthology or encyclopedia, in which the Work in its entirety in unmodified form, along with a number of other contributions, constituting separate and independent works in themselves, are assembled into a collective whole. A work that constitutes a Collective Work will not be considered a Derivative Work (as defined below) for the purposes of this Licence.
   b **"Derivative Work"** means a work based upon the Work or upon the Work and other pre-existing works, such as a musical arrangement, dramatization, fictionalization, motion picture version, sound recording, art reproduction, abridgment, condensation, or any other form in which the Work may be recast, transformed, or adapted, except that a work that constitutes a Collective Work or a translation from English into another language will not be considered a Derivative Work for the purpose of this Licence.
   c **"Licensor"** means the individual or entity that offers the Work under the terms of this Licence.
   d **"Original Author"** means the individual or entity who created the Work.
   e **"Work"** means the copyrightable work of authorship offered under the terms of this Licence.
   f **"You"** means an individual or entity exercising rights under this Licence who has not previously violated the terms of this Licence with respect to the Work, or who has received express permission from DEMOS to exercise rights under this Licence despite a previous violation.
2. **Fair Use Rights.** Nothing in this licence is intended to reduce, limit, or restrict any rights arising from fair use, first sale or other limitations on the exclusive rights of the copyright owner under copyright law or other applicable laws.
3. **Licence Grant.** Subject to the terms and conditions of this Licence, Licensor hereby grants You a worldwide, royalty-free, non-exclusive, perpetual (for the duration of the applicable copyright) licence to exercise the rights in the Work as stated below:
   a to reproduce the Work, to incorporate the Work into one or more Collective Works, and to reproduce the Work as incorporated in the Collective Works;
   b to distribute copies or phonorecords of, display publicly, perform publicly, and perform publicly by means of a digital audio transmission the Work including as incorporated in Collective Works;
   The above rights may be exercised in all media and formats whether now known or hereafter devised. The above rights include the right to make such modifications as are technically necessary to exercise the rights in other media and formats. All rights not expressly granted by Licensor are hereby reserved.
4. **Restrictions.** The licence granted in Section 3 above is expressly made subject to and limited by the following restrictions:
   a You may distribute, publicly display, publicly perform, or publicly digitally perform the Work only under the terms of this Licence, and You must include a copy of, or the Uniform Resource Identifier for, this Licence with every copy or phonorecord of the Work You distribute, publicly display, publicly perform, or publicly digitally perform. You may not offer or impose any terms on the Work that alter or restrict the terms of this Licence or the recipients' exercise of the rights granted hereunder. You may not sublicence the Work. You must keep intact all notices that refer to this Licence and to the disclaimer of warranties. You may not distribute, publicly display, publicly perform, or publicly digitally perform the Work with any technological measures that control access or use of the Work in a manner inconsistent with the terms of this Licence Agreement. The above applies to the Work as incorporated in a Collective Work, but this does not require the Collective Work apart from the Work itself to be made subject to the terms of this Licence. If You create a Collective Work, upon notice from any Licencor You must, to the extent practicable, remove from the Collective Work any reference to such Licensor or the Original Author, as requested.
   b You may not exercise any of the rights granted to You in Section 3 above in any manner that is primarily intended for or directed toward commercial advantage or private monetary

compensation. The exchange of the Work for other copyrighted works by means of digital file-sharing or otherwise shall not be considered to be intended for or directed toward commercial advantage or private monetary compensation, provided there is no payment of any monetary compensation in connection with the exchange of copyrighted works.

    **c**  If you distribute, publicly display, publicly perform, or publicly digitally perform the Work or any Collective Works, You must keep intact all copyright notices for the Work and give the Original Author credit reasonable to the medium or means You are utilizing by conveying the name (or pseudonym if applicable) of the Original Author if supplied; the title of the Work if supplied. Such credit may be implemented in any reasonable manner; provided, however, that in the case of a Collective Work, at a minimum such credit will appear where any other comparable authorship credit appears and in a manner at least as prominent as such other comparable authorship credit.

**5. Representations, Warranties and Disclaimer**

    **a**  By offering the Work for public release under this Licence, Licensor represents and warrants that, to the best of Licensor's knowledge after reasonable inquiry:

        **i**  Licensor has secured all rights in the Work necessary to grant the licence rights hereunder and to permit the lawful exercise of the rights granted hereunder without You having any obligation to pay any royalties, compulsory licence fees, residuals or any other payments;

        **ii**  The Work does not infringe the copyright, trademark, publicity rights, common law rights or any other right of any third party or constitute defamation, invasion of privacy or other tortious injury to any third party.

    **b**  EXCEPT AS EXPRESSLY STATED IN THIS LICENCE OR OTHERWISE AGREED IN WRITING OR REQUIRED BY APPLICABLE LAW, THE WORK IS LICENCED ON AN "AS IS" BASIS, WITHOUT WARRANTIES OF ANY KIND, EITHER EXPRESS OR IMPLIED INCLUDING, WITHOUT LIMITATION, ANY WARRANTIES REGARDING THE CONTENTS OR ACCURACY OF THE WORK.

**6. Limitation on Liability.** EXCEPT TO THE EXTENT REQUIRED BY APPLICABLE LAW, AND EXCEPT FOR DAMAGES ARISING FROM LIABILITY TO A THIRD PARTY RESULTING FROM BREACH OF THE WARRANTIES IN SECTION 5, IN NO EVENT WILL LICENSOR BE LIABLE TO YOU ON ANY LEGAL THEORY FOR ANY SPECIAL, INCIDENTAL, CONSEQUENTIAL, PUNITIVE OR EXEMPLARY DAMAGES ARISING OUT OF THIS LICENCE OR THE USE OF THE WORK, EVEN IF LICENSOR HAS BEEN ADVISED OF THE POSSIBILITY OF SUCH DAMAGES.

**7. Termination**

    **a**  This Licence and the rights granted hereunder will terminate automatically upon any breach by You of the terms of this Licence. Individuals or entities who have received Collective Works from You under this Licence, however, will not have their licences terminated provided such individuals or entities remain in full compliance with those licences. Sections 1, 2, 5, 6, 7, and 8 will survive any termination of this Licence.

    **b**  Subject to the above terms and conditions, the licence granted here is perpetual (for the duration of the applicable copyright in the Work). Notwithstanding the above, Licensor reserves the right to release the Work under different licence terms or to stop distributing the Work at any time; provided, however that any such election will not serve to withdraw this Licence (or any other licence that has been, or is required to be, granted under the terms of this Licence), and this Licence will continue in full force and effect unless terminated as stated above.

8. Miscellaneous

    **a**  Each time You distribute or publicly digitally perform the Work or a Collective Work, DEMOS offers to the recipient a licence to the Work on the same terms and conditions as the licence granted to You under this Licence.

    **b**  If any provision of this Licence is invalid or unenforceable under applicable law, it shall not affect the validity or enforceability of the remainder of the terms of this Licence, and without further action by the parties to this agreement, such provision shall be reformed to the minimum extent necessary to make such provision valid and enforceable.

    **c**  No term or provision of this Licence shall be deemed waived and no breach consented to unless such waiver or consent shall be in writing and signed by the party to be charged with such waiver or consent.

    **d**  This Licence constitutes the entire agreement between the parties with respect to the Work licensed here. There are no understandings, agreements or representations with respect to the Work not specified here. Licensor shall not be bound by any additional provisions that may appear in any communication from You. This Licence may not be modified without the mutual written agreement of DEMOS and You.